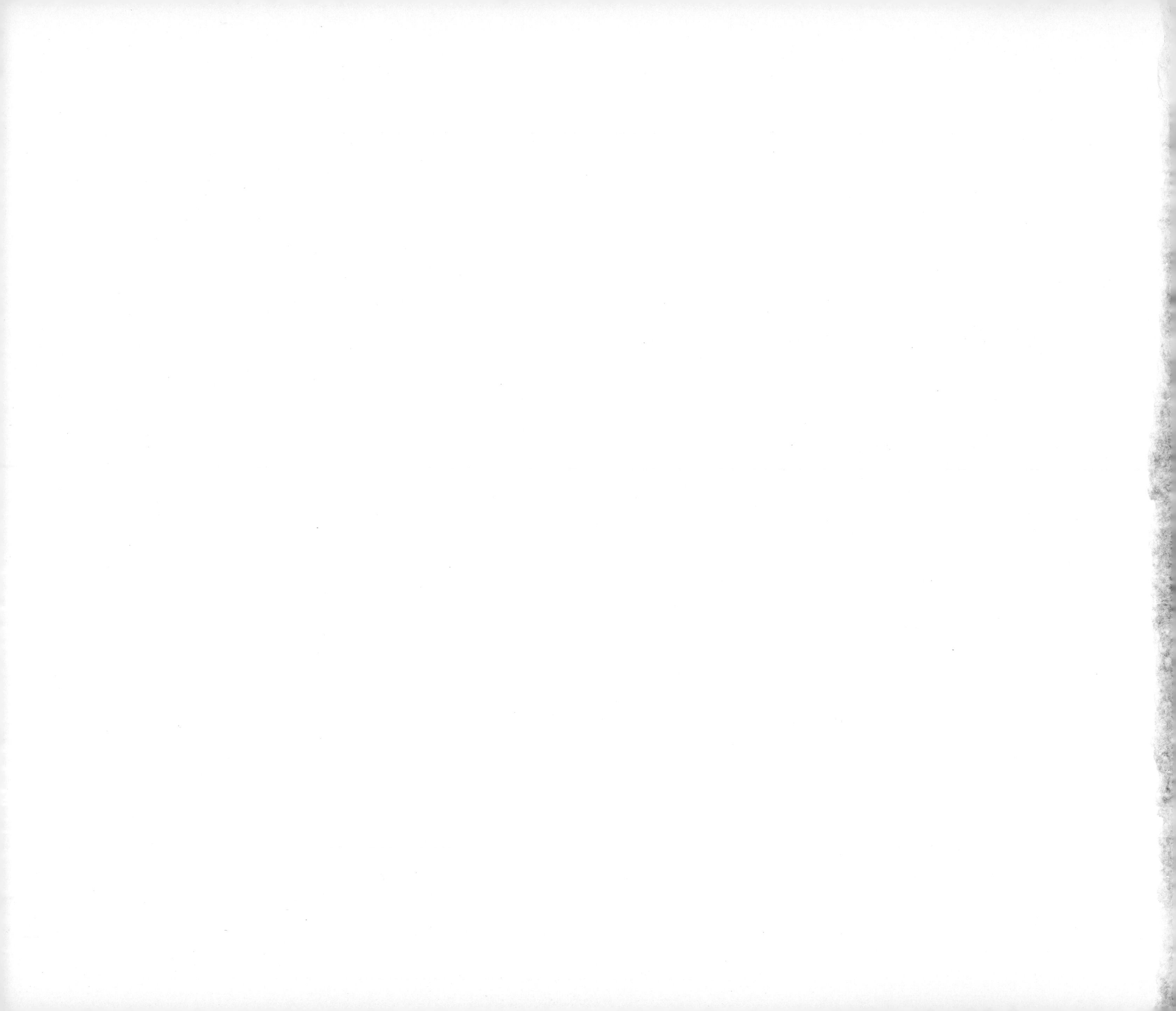

THE MAN WITH THE
GOLDEN EYE

POS PROJECTOR
825
825
825
501
473
CINEMASCOPE 2·55
ALBERT R. BROCCOLI and HARRY SALTZMAN present
ROGER MOORE as
JAMES BOND 007
in IAN FLEMING'S
LIVE AND LET DIE
Directed by GUY HAMILTON
the
story
behind
james
bond
007's
world
record
boat
leap
BOAT CHASE
List of Glastron Boats to be used during chase.
Boat Type
GT 150
CV 19
V 162 Futura
V 145 Fireflite
V 156 Sportster
V 162 Futura
HARRY SALTZMAN & ALBERT R. BROCCOLI
PRESENT
SEAN CONNERY
as JAMES BOND 007
in IAN FLEMING'S
YOU ONLY LIVE TWICE
Directed by
LEWIS GILBERT
TECHNICOLOR®
PANAVISION®
AN EON PRODUCTION
Released through UNITED ARTISTS
MILITARY INTELLIGE
MI6 SECURITY S
THIS DISC MUST NOT LEAVE TH
DIVISION
ALBERT R. BROCCOLI
presents
ROGER MOORE
as IAN FLEMING'S
JAMES BOND OO
IN
FOR YOUR EYES ON
PRODUCED BY ALBERT R. BROCCOLI DIRECTED BY JOHN G
EXECUTIVE PRODUCER MICHAEL G. WILSON
ROYAL WORLD CHARITY PREMIERE
IN THE PRESENCE OF
PRINCE OF WALES K.G.
JAMES BOND 007
MOONRAKER
PRE TITLE
OPENING
19
2ND UNIT
STUDIO
WHIRRRR...
POSSIBLE INSERT?
CABLE being REELED in...
35
CUT
1ST UNIT
STUDIO
BOND is pulled gently down thro' frame
36
CUT
LT. M'S OFFICE · HERCULES

THE MAN WITH THE GOLDEN EYE

PETER LAMONT
with MARCUS HEARN

SIGNUM BOOKS

For Ann,
my dear wife of 63 years

This edition published in Great Britain in 2016 by Signum Books,
an imprint of
Flashpoint Media Ltd
173 Mill Road
Cambridge
CB1 3AN

A CIP catalogue record for this book is available from the British Library.

ISBN 978 0 9955191 1 4

Designed by Mike Jones

Printed and bound in China by 1010 Printing International Ltd.

Most of the pictures in this book are from the author's private collection. In addition, the author and publishers would like to thank Eon Productions, MGM and United Artists for permission to reproduce images from the following films:

Above: A prop designed for *The Ipcress File* in 1964 and subsequently used in the James Bond film *Thunderball*.

CONTENTS

INTRODUCTION

So many members of my family have been artists and designers that I sometimes wonder whether this creative instinct is in the Lamont genes.

I was born in 1929. My father Cyril and his brother Lionel, commonly known as Bill, were both signwriters in an era before basic graphic aids like Letraset even existed. As a child I would gaze in awe as my father spent hours painting letters on the side of a van. When he finished, my mother, Mabel, would join him outside and complete the job by gilding his artwork. The result was immaculate, and it was all achieved with nothing more sophisticated than a chalk guideline, a pencil and a brush.

We lived in Borehamwood, north of London, and my father often worked at the local British and Dominion film studio. Nobody had permanent jobs in those days; people would gather at the gates of the various Borehamwood studios and wait for the head carpenter or someone like that to select them for a day's employment.

My father's signwriting skills were so unusual that he was often picked for work. Sometimes a telegram would arrive at our home in Beach Drive, summoning him to B and D for several days. There'd be no time to come home, so he'd bed down in the art department overnight.

In 1936 a fire destroyed the three stages at B and D, so my father found work at Denham Studios and the recently opened Pinewood Studios. Shortly afterwards we moved to a house nearby. I looked up to my father, and as I got older I started to draw at home. He'd bring old scripts back from work and I'd use them as sketch pads. When I realised how difficult it was to emulate his style I developed an even deeper respect for his artistry.

Opposite page: On the Pinewood backlot, measuring the lavish sets for *Cleopatra* (1963).

Above left: Smiling for the camera, aged four.

Above right: My father Cyril, screen printing in a page from a brochure published to promote MGM's Borehamwood studio.

Below left: Other members of the Lamont family who worked in the film business included my cousin Alan Maley. Alan was a scenic and matte artist as well as a painter. He won an Academy Award for his work on Disney's *Bedknobs and Broomsticks* in 1972.

Below centre: John Lamont was another of my cousins. John was a scenic artist and master painter.

Below right: My brother Michael was a master modeller and art director.

I was an only child until my brother Michael came along in 1939. In time, he would develop his own artistic talents.

When war broke out I continued my education at the makeshift school in our local village hall. Unfortunately I didn't get through the 11-Plus, the examination that supposedly decided if I was smart enough for a grammar school education.

I became intrigued by my father's activities at Denham, and I vividly remember the first time he invited me onto a film set. In 1942 he took me behind the scenes on Michael Powell and Emeric Pressburger's drama *One of Our Aircraft is Missing*. It was thrilling to climb aboard a real Wellington bomber, but later that day I was equally excited to discover a workshop where a miniature Wellington was being made for one of the special effects sequences.

Other distractions included the cinema. Tickets were cheap, and my mother would take me to the Regal in Uxbridge every week.

Back at school I did well in my 13-Plus exam and won a scholarship to High Wycombe Technical Institute. This provided me with a foundation for the skills I would take into my working life, and during my subsequent visits to Denham I grew increasingly curious about life behind the huge doors of the soundstages. In those days I aspired to the camera department – which I considered to be more glamorous than my father's art department – but the allure of filmmaking in general had me under its spell.

In 1945 I saw Claude Rains and Vivien Leigh on the sumptuous set of *Caesar and Cleopatra*, touted at the time as the "The biggest picture ever made". A year later I watched from a corner of the studio as Powell and Pressburger filmed their classic *A Matter of Life and Death*. In America the film was renamed *Stairway to Heaven*, and I even had a ride on the huge staircase that production designer Alfred Junge constructed on Stage 4 at Denham.

When I graduated from High Wycombe, my father got me a job as an assistant print boy and runner in Edward Carrick's art department. I would cycle around the studio, delivering copies of set drawings to the workshops and stages. Teddy had founded England's first film school

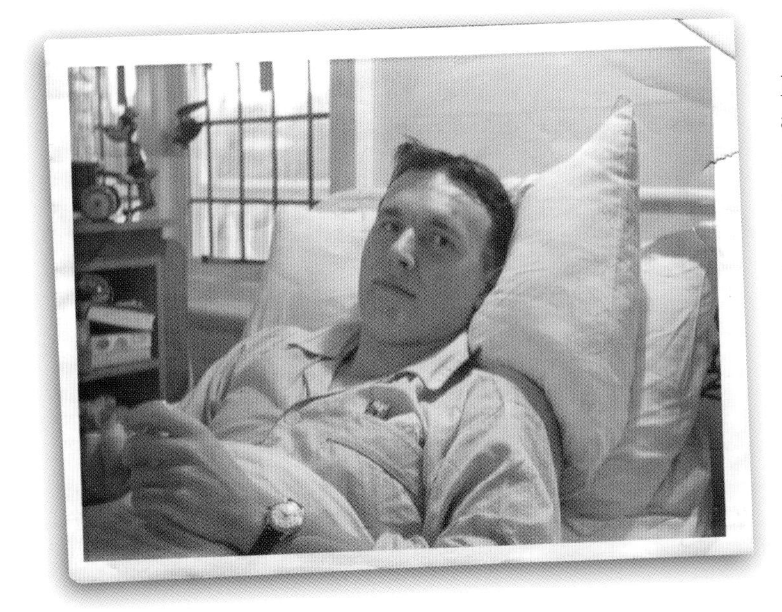

before the war. He was happy to share his wisdom, and I was glad he took me under his wing.

Teddy must have had faith in me, because one day I was given a drawing board, an adjustable set square and some pencils. During the production of *Captain Boycott* in 1947 I made my first professional drawing. Teddy asked me to illustrate a Georgian house, and although this was an exercise rather than a piece of actual set design for the film, I felt as though I'd taken an important first step.

Later that year production designer Peter Proud asked me to contribute my first actual designs, for the Jean Simmons film *The Woman in the Hall*. You didn't get to draw a full-blown set until you'd paid your dues. I was nowhere near attaining that status, but I was pleased to have contributed some small details.

In February 1948 the time came for me to begin my National Service. The two years and nine days I spent in the Royal Air Force taught me a lot of practical engineering skills, and after I trained to become a mechanic on airframes I was posted to RAF Fairford in Gloucestershire and then RAF North Luffenham in Rutland. A detachment to Malta gave me my first trip abroad.

The law stated that demobbed servicemen had to be reinstated to their old jobs, so in 1950 I returned to Pinewood and picked up where I'd left off as a junior draughtsman. My new salary was £7 10 shillings a week – a lot of money to almost any young man at that time.

In 1952 I married Ann Aldridge, a beautiful girl I'd known since I was at school, and we moved into a flat opposite Denham Station. That year I worked with art director Carmen Dillon on *The Importance of Being Earnest*. The film's draughtsmen included Ernest Archer, John Box and Jack Stephens, all of whom would go on to win Oscars in later life. In Jack's case, he won four.

Two years later I was promoted to draughtsman, which meant I was finally allowed to design sets. Ernie had become something of a mentor to me, and I looked to him for inspiration. He would arrive in the morning with a cigarette hanging out of his mouth, take off his duffel coat, hat, scarf and gloves and knock out one masterpiece after another.

Top left: In hospital, recovering from an operation in the 1950s.

Above: Pages from the book published to celebrate the release of *A Matter of Life and Death* in 1946.

Left: The scaffolding holding up the staircase at Denham Studios. *A Matter of Life and Death* is still my favourite film.

Right and far right: Pictures from the Pinewood filming of *Cleopatra*. The figures in the foreground on the left are director of photography Jack Hildyard and director Rouben Mamoulian. Neither would be credited on the finished film.

Below: The sets for *Cleopatra* engulfed the Pinewood backlot.

By 1961 Ann and I had two children, Madelaine and Neil, so we moved to a larger house in Iver Heath, near Pinewood. I was now a set dresser, working on the television series *Interpol Calling* (1959-60), and a several pictures, including *The Bulldog Breed* (1960) and the lavish *Cleopatra* (1963). These were some of the biggest sets that I, or indeed anybody, had ever dressed. During the film's troubled occupation of Pinewood I met someone else who would become an inspiration to me. Production designer John DeCuir was one of the nicest and cleverest men I ever worked with.

Waltz of the Toreadors (1962) was the last film I worked on at Pinewood before moving to Beaconsfield Studios. Here I joined the art departments of *Crooks Anonymous* (1962), *The Fast Lady* (1962) and Lindsay Anderson's intimate drama *This Sporting Life* (1963). Leading man Richard Harris was a superb actor, but he was also a notorious drinker whose hellraising habits caused a few problems. I was on set one day when, during a very difficult scene, Richard exploded with rage. The air turned blue for five minutes until Lindsay said, "Shall we do the scene again?" He remained calm, but he was on the verge of quitting. He told me, "If I'm not here on Monday, Karel [Reisz] might be taking over."

At the end of shooting on Friday, the first assistant wished everybody a good weekend. Before we left, Richard raised his hand and announced, "I'm so sorry for the way I spoke to Lindsay, whose birthday it is today." Then a bunch of caterers appeared, and Richard treated us all to Champagne

and canapés. I came away from *This Sporting Life* with a great admiration for him, and my first on-screen credit.

In those days the British film industry offered a diverse array of entertainment, and

I thought nothing of going from a Roman epic to a kitchen sink drama. In 1963 *Father Came Too!* gave me the chance to work with comedy stars such as James Robertson Justice, Leslie Phillips and Stanley Baxter. If one of the main sets seemed familiar it was because I'd already dressed it the previous year on *The Fast Lady*.

I didn't know it at the time, but I was about to join a very special family of filmmakers and contribute to a remarkable series of pictures. Over the following chapters I'll explain how I was promoted to art director and ultimately production designer, and how I tried to bring something different to every film I made. The only predictable part is a commitment to detail and authenticity that is a thread through all the globetrotting adventures I'm going to recount.

Along the way I'll pay tribute to some of the great talents I worked with, including many of the back room boys and girls who are overdue a bit of credit. To any friends and colleagues I may neglect to mention, my apologies. I'm getting on a bit now, so a few oversights are probably inevitable.

People have often asked me about my experiences on the James Bond films. This is how I remember it...

Far left: Richard Harris (as Frank Machin) and William Hartnell (as 'Dad' Johnson) in *This Sporting Life* (1963). Albert Fennell, who was in charge of the production, gave me my first screen credit on this film.

Left: A portrait from the early 1960s.

Below left: Stanley Baxter (as Murdoch Troon) and James Robertson Justice (as Charles Chingford), behind the wheel of *The Fast Lady* (1962).

Below right: The cottage in Hedgerley, Buckinghamshire, where we filmed *Father Came Too!* (1964).

GOLDFINGER

My career in the James Bond films started with a phone call in 1963. I was glad to hear the familiar voice of Peter Murton, an art director I'd known for years.

"Would you be interested in working on a picture called *Goldfinger*?" asked Peter. I had an empty diary, so I'd have been interested in almost anything. "I've already got a set decorator," he continued, "but if you'd like to do some draughting for us, you've got the job."

I hadn't actually seen the first two films in the series, but I found out that *From Russia With Love* was currently playing in Slough. I joined the queue at the Granada cinema in Windsor Street and settled down to see what all the fuss was about. I was deeply impressed by the scenes shot in the garden at Pinewood Studios, the glamour of the Istanbul setting and the ferocious punch-up between Bond (Sean Connery) and Red Grant (Robert Shaw) on the train. The sheer variety of props was also a little overwhelming. The film was co-produced by Albert 'Cubby' Broccoli, and when I got to know him I discovered that this was his favourite Bond film. Looking back on it, I can see why.

From Russia With Love was fresh in my mind when I reported to assistant art director Maurice Pelling at Pinewood. Peter was the art director and the department was led by the charismatic Ken Adam, who was the production designer.

Ken took a large cigar out of his mouth and asked if I was aware of his reputation. Although I had yet to see *Dr No*, I knew it wasn't the only good picture he'd made; he'd also worked on *The Crimson Pirate* (1952) and Cubby's film *The Trials of Oscar Wilde* (1960).

He handed me a wodge of photographs and said, "See what you can do with this." Spreading the pictures out in front of me I could see that Ken had visited Fort Knox, the US government's bullion depository in Kentucky. For obvious reasons, Ken's reconnaissance trip hadn't extended to a guided tour, but the pictures clearly showed the exterior behind the high, imposing gates. There was no question of shooting *Goldfinger*'s climactic scenes in the real thing, so it would be our job to create an authentic-looking set based on Ken's photographs and the approximate measurements included in some blurb that he also gave me.

Opposite page: Sean Connery as James Bond, outside the Fort Knox set on the Pinewood backlot.

Top: The front of the Fort Knox set.

Above: A picture of me, standing outside the main entrance.

Above left: Goldfinger's guards outside Fort Knox.

Top right: My brother Michael parked his car in front of the set to help me judge the scale.

Above right: A location shot from the film, showing Pussy Galore's Flying Circus over the real Fort Knox in Kentucky.

I reached for my dividers and spent the next month on the drawings, beginning with a rough sketch of the facade. Once I had that looking right, I made more detailed drawings of the exterior, including the doors, the fencing and the roads, the last of which were due to be constructed at Black Park, near Pinewood. Every now and then Ken would look over my shoulder to see how I was getting on, and when I was finished he used my drawings to get a quote. The estimate came in at £65,000, which in 1963 was a huge amount of money to spend on a single exterior set.

A commitment of this size needed to be authorised at the highest level, so Cubby Broccoli decided to discuss the expenditure with his co-producer Harry Saltzman. I didn't know either of them particularly well at this time, but it soon became clear that they had very different personalities. Harry was the frantic one; if you went to his office you'd find him being measured for a suit while trying to answer three or four phones at the same time. Cubby always seemed quite calm and serene by comparison.

Cubby, Harry and the director Guy Hamilton came over to the art department to discuss the budget. Guy examined a model we'd made, and asked if we could cut the sides off the set to economise. By creating just the back and the front of Fort Knox, with returns but no actual sides, we were able to bring the bill down to £47,000. This was still an awful lot of money, but we were told that we should go ahead and spend it, on the proviso that we didn't go over that budget.

Two or three weeks later Ken came up to my desk and asked me if I'd been to D Stage, where the walls of the set and the other elements were being constructed. "You should go and have a look," he said, with a note of concern in his voice. "I think something's wrong..."

I immediately headed for D Stage, where I was confronted by the facade of Fort Knox in all its gigantic glory. The set must have been 25 feet high and 120 feet long, practically filling the entire stage. Ken told me it was far too big, and as I stared at the walls towering over me in this confined space I started to wonder if I'd made a terrible mistake. When I got back to my desk I took my divider to the drawings and told Ken that everything seemed to be correct. "Are you *sure*?" he asked, in a voice that suggested he wasn't entirely convinced. "I hope it will look all right when there are people and cars in front of it..." I promised him the set would look smaller when it was out in the open, but privately I was starting to panic.

At Black Park the contractors had already laid new concrete roads that matched the pictures of Gold Vault Road and Bullion Boulevard that Ken had brought back from Kentucky. On the Pinewood backlot, trees were being moved into position so the setting for our version of Fort Knox would look as authentic as possible.

By this time my younger brother Michael had joined me in the art department, also working as a draughtsman. When the set went up I asked him to bring his car to the backlot so we could park in the same position as the cars in Ken's photographs. That way I felt I could prove once and for all that we'd built the Fort Knox set to the

BELOW: Harry Saltzman (right) was one of the producers who authorised the budget for the Fort Knox set. Here he inspects the results.

Right: Michael on the set of Goldfinger's Lockheed JetStar.

Far right: Members of the art department finishing props inside the plane.

Below: Bond and Mei-Lei (Mai Ling) aboard Goldfinger's plane.

correct scale. We stepped back from our cars and I examined everything through a viewfinder. It all looked fine, but I still couldn't shake the nagging doubt that I'd been somehow responsible for wasting £47,000...

To add to my insecurity, Maurice told me that the art department was about to be slimmed down. "You'd better see if you can get another job," he said. "I'll be all right – I'm well in here." Now convinced that my days with Cubby and Harry's Eon Productions were numbered, I decided to accept an offer to work on the television series *Danger Man* in Borehamwood. I went to see Peter, explaining that I was going to leave before I was pushed. I was surprised by his response. "Oh no you don't," he said. "We've got a big programme here and you're needed. Besides, Ken likes you."

"You could have fooled me," I replied, revealing my concern over the dimensions of Fort Knox. Peter's face broke into a broad grin. "Every time Ken says anything like that you bite. We were laughing ourselves silly when you went down to D Stage. You knew it was fine, but then you went running up to the lot with your brother and a bloody viewfinder!" The whole thing had been one long, protracted joke at my expense.

I took it all in good humour, but the rumours of job losses persisted. One Thursday Maurice came up to me and said, "Have you had a letter yet?" He was convinced that I was about to receive my notice. I only lived about 100 yards down the road from the studio, so at lunchtime I dashed home to check. "What are you doing here?" asked Ann, my wife. "Has anything arrived for me in the post?" I asked. "No," she said, looking confused. The same thing happened on Friday. On Monday afternoon I once again returned to work empty-handed. This time I was met by Maurice, who was clutching a letter. "What's that?" I asked. "It's my notice," he replied, ashen-faced.

FAR LEFT: Two of Ken Adam's most impressive sets. Goldfinger's 'rumpus room'...

LEFT: ... and the interior of Fort Knox. Cubby Broccoli described this as "a cathedral of gold".

BELOW: An advertisement for the film's premiere in September 1964.

Maurice was a good draughtsman, but he could be difficult and I don't think Ken liked him. Maurice won an Oscar for *Cleopatra* (1963) and bringing it into the office didn't help. As soon as Ken saw it he said, "What's that bloody thing?" Sadly, Maurice was working on a film in Spain in 1973 when he was killed in a car accident.

I stayed with *Goldfinger* until we finished, five months later. Work on Fort Knox continued with the interior sets. Peter drew many of these designs himself and asked me to assist him with the details. We'd been careful to ensure the exterior looked authentic, but the interior was a figment of Ken's imagination. Here was a heavily guarded bank vault containing 15 billion dollars' worth of bullion – a cathedral of gold. Meanwhile my brother worked on the interior of Bond's Aston Martin DB5 – a customised vehicle that would go down in history as the greatest of all the James Bond cars.

Goldfinger was released in September 1964 and its incredible success was due in no small part to Ken Adam's vision and ingenuity. Before he came along, British art departments were very mediocre compared to their American counterparts. Ken had started in a relatively minor way on *Dr No* because he was restricted by that film's budget, but the laser room – where Goldfinger (Gert Fröbe) tortures the captive 007 – and the 'rumpus room' – where he illustrates his grand ambitions to the assembled gangsters – really showed what could be achieved in this country. Audiences had never seen sets like this before, and it's a pity Ken's work on this film wasn't recognised with an Academy Award.

I was only an uncredited draughtsman on *Goldfinger*, but I was proud to be part of the art department and grateful that Eon Productions asked me to stay on. The end titles promised that James Bond would be back, and I certainly hoped to be there when that happened.

THUNDERBALL

I was working on *The Ipcress File* in autumn 1964 when Ken swept into the art department and announced, "Children – we're going to do *Thunderball*. Somebody had better learn to swim underwater!"

The story concerned the theft of two NATO atomic bombs by the sinister SPECTRE organisation. The bombs are stolen from a hijacked Vulcan bomber and then held to ransom for £100 million in diamonds. An unprecedented amount of the action, including the actual theft, would be filmed underwater, mostly in the clear seas off the Bahamas. This was territory familiar to Kevin McClory, co-author of the original story and our producer. In order to prevent McClory making *Thunderball* as a rival Bond film, Cubby and Harry took a back seat on this one, acting as executive producers.

Before my thoughts turned to the Bahamas, I spent much of the winter at Pinewood, planning the sets for the Vulcan bomber sequences in my capacity as chief draughtsman. My experience in the RAF came in useful, and we gathered as much technical literature as we could to make sure that both the exterior and the interior of the aircraft were accurate.

Peter Twist, our liaison at the Ministry of Defence, offered to take us to RAF Waddington in Lincolnshire where he said we'd be able to photograph the bomb bay of a Vulcan B2. We were examining the underside of the plane when we heard a phone ring in the dispersal bay. The squadron leader answered the call and then dashed back to explain that he'd been refused permission to open the bomb doors after all. He didn't explain why, but I suspected the plane was armed. By way of consolation, he told us that if we stayed for a short while we'd see something impressive. Sure enough, four Vulcans were scrambled for a two-minute take off, all roaring into the sky above us at the same time. It was a spectacular sight.

We still needed to see inside a Vulcan bomb bay, however, so Peter arranged for us to visit the School of Technical Training at RAF Halton.

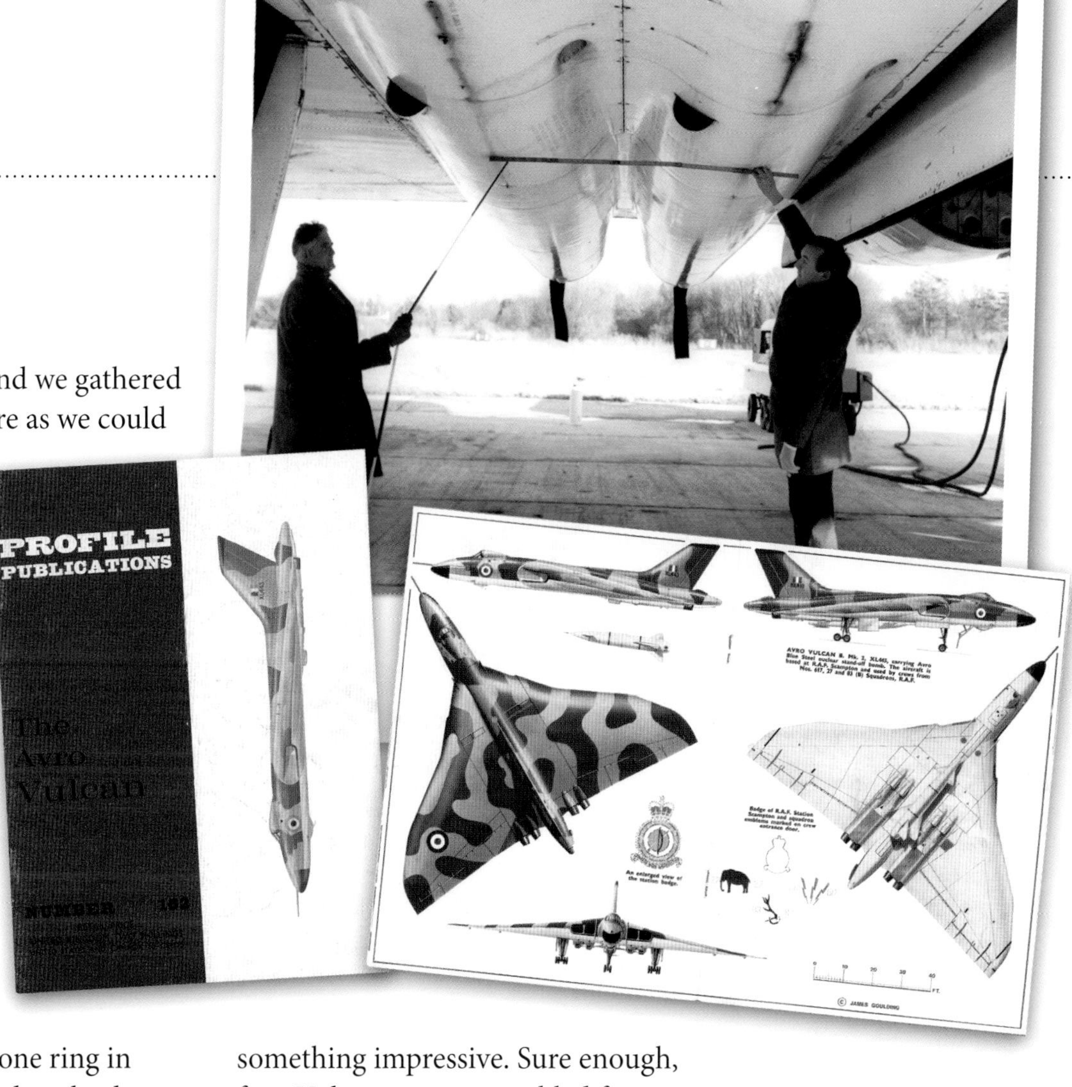

Opposite page: Building the full-size Vulcan at Paradise Island in the Bahamas.

Top: With my art department colleague Ronnie Udell (left), measuring the underside of a Vulcan at RAF Halton.

Above: Some of the reference literature I gathered during my research for *Thunderball*.

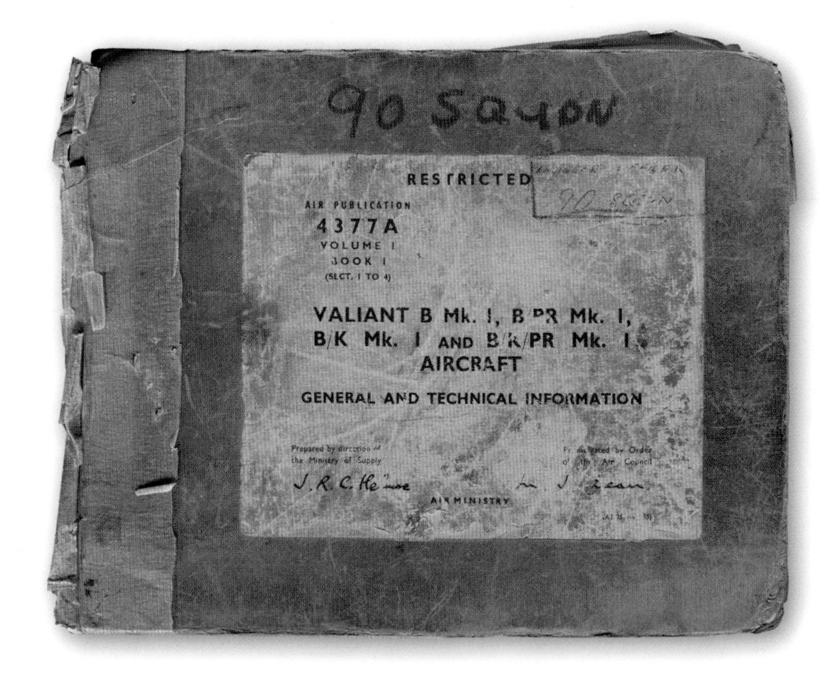
90 SQDN

RESTRICTED

AIR PUBLICATION
4377A
VOLUME I
BOOK I
(SECT. I TO 4)

VALIANT B Mk. I, B PR Mk. I,
B/K Mk. I AND B/K/PR Mk. I
AIRCRAFT

GENERAL AND TECHNICAL INFORMATION

AIR MINISTRY

Above: An example of the Valiant technical information given to me by the staff at RAF Honington.

Below left: The imposter Palazzi (Paul Stassino, left) takes his place in the Vulcan bomber.

Below right: Another view of the set, which was based on the cockpit of a Valiant.

We met a squadron leader called Dennis Mountford, and the staff at the school opened up the bomb bay of a Vulcan B1, allowing us to look inside. They even let us mould the plane's air intakes in plaster. They then showed us a pressure cabin that they displayed at exhibitions. We asked to take this back to Pinewood, where we made moulds of the entire thing. While looking around their dumping area one of the technical staff found two bomb racks from a Valiant, which was the original V bomber. We took those back to Pinewood as well, promising to return them when we'd finished.

My brother Michael joined me for a weekend, during which we drew the plans for the quarter-sized Vulcan model that was to be constructed by special effects supervisor John Stears. We knew early on that the Vulcan would be filmed on the sea bed with pilots inside, so there was no alternative but to also make a full-size set. In addition, we made another Vulcan model at eighth scale. The sequence of the Vulcan landing on the water, sinking beneath the waves and coming to rest on the sea bed was filmed using a combination of all three. The full-sized Vulcan would be built in the Bahamas but the others were built at Pinewood before being shipped out.

In January 1965 I read in a Sunday newspaper that the RAF had decided to retire its Valiant bombers. I called Peter Twist and asked him if we could get hold of one. He explained that he thought they'd all been broken up for scrap, but that he'd see what he could do for us. I next heard from Dennis Mountford, who suggested we visited RAF Honington in Suffolk, where there'd be something waiting for us. There we found the near-complete body of a Valiant – the classified instruments had been stripped out of the pressure cabin, but everything else was intact. We paid the MOD £3,000 for the bomb doors and the pressure cabin, which were delivered to Pinewood.

The Valiant's fuselage number, XD814, revealed that this had been the first V bomber to drop bombs in anger, on Egypt during the Suez Crisis. Its sister plane, XD816, had dropped a thermonuclear bomb on Christmas Island. The technical staff at Honington asked if I would like the Valiant's service manual, and they gave me Volume III. Reading it overnight, I realised that what I actually needed was Volume IV, which included details on nuclear weapons. Honington initially said they would forward a copy to me but soon changed their minds when they realised it was restricted.

Norman Reynolds, one of my fellow draughtsmen, did a brilliant job of making the interior of the Valiant look

like a Vulcan, based on our photographs, drawings and the moulds we'd already made. In the end we only had to manufacture one instrument for our Vulcan cockpit – a meter showing the position of the flight controls.

Despite all this, we knew our Vulcan interior wasn't entirely accurate. There's no connecting door, for example, between the pressure cabin and bomb bay on the real thing, but we had to add one because the script required Bond (Sean Connery) to gain access to the cockpit via the open bomb doors when he discovered the submerged plane.

Every time I met Dennis Mountford I bombarded him with questions. One day he invited Ken and I to the officers' mess at RAF Strike Command in Naphill. After dinner we were taken to the war room. As he ushered us inside, Dennis said, "All of the answers to your questions are hanging on these walls."

The stolen bombs were made at Pinewood, based on what I'd been shown – but hadn't been allowed to photograph – in the war room at Naphill. By memorising the details on those pictures I was able to ensure that the wording on each of our prop bombs was exactly as it should have been. The tow sleds used to get the bombs away from the plane's bomb bay were designed by Ken and built by a guy called Jordan Klein in Miami.

While I was collecting material for the Vulcan, the search was on for the *Disco Volante*, the heavily armed hydrofoil owned by SPECTRE agent Emilio Largo (Adolfo Celi). The original plan was to adapt a high-speed boat built by Denison for the American Navy. We prepared drawings showing where the prop foils should be attached and made a model which Ken took to the US. It soon became obvious, however, that it wasn't going to work – although fast, the Denison was a large boat and the length of the fins would have given us trouble in the shallow waters of Nassau.

The boat that was eventually chosen was found by Ken and Peter Murton in Puerto Rico. *The Flying Fish* was a much smaller vessel and a genuine hydrofoil.

Above: The bomb bay and incongruous door from the full-size Vulcan set.

Below left: Posing as the captain of *The Flying Fish*.

Below right: A shot of the foils from the deck of *The Flying Fish*.

Above left: At the dock in Paradise Island.
Above centre: With my brother Michael, in our wetsuits.
Above right: On board *The Flying Fish*.

It was, however, fairly dilapidated, so they took it to Miami where it was renovated by a yacht brokerage called Allied Marine.

Towards the end of the film, the *Disco Volante* jettisons its rear cocoon section and speeds away from the pursuing US Navy ships with Bond clinging to one of its foils. We designed the cocoon at Pinewood, where there were concerns that it would split apart like a banana. To ensure the best job possible we sent the plans to the experts at Allied Marine, where Michael had now joined Peter. For the underside of the boat we designed a compartment with double-doors that opened to reveal Largo's mini-submarine and the SPECTRE frogmen.

As the various elements started to arrive in the Bahamas, Ken told me he needed someone to go down there to keep an eye on things. Remembering Ken's advice at the beginning of pre-production, I decided to enrol in scuba diving classes. Michael and I signed up for a crash course at a local club, where we were put through something called 'the ordeal'. You swim down to the bottom of a pool and find a weight-belt which you have to put on. Then you have to find your regulator and valve, turn it on, put the mouthpiece in, put your mask on and clear it, then put on your backpack and swim up to the surface. Once I was comfortable doing all that I felt I was ready.

In March 1965 I took a Trans World flight to the Bahamas via New York, in the company of assistant art director Michael White and some of the other crew members. I'd been told the job would take a fortnight, and because this was my first foreign location shoot I believed it. Filming the underwater Vulcan would actually take 14 weeks.

At Nassau I checked into the Yacht Club and arranged to meet the crew members who had already arrived, including assistant art director Robert Laing. Many of them were staying at a nearby hotel, but Ken and his wife Letizia had a place on Love Beach, where Sean Connery and his wife Diane Cilento were also staying.

We were due to make our base on Paradise Island, just off the shore of Nassau. Nowadays Paradise Island is connected to the town by a couple of bridges, but the first of these wouldn't be built until 1966. We reached the island on a ferry which we caught outside the Mermaid Tavern. Once we got our bearings, we gathered at Hurricane Hole Marina to assemble the equipment that was arriving from Pinewood and Miami. Inside the containers and packages were the tools we'd need to build the Vulcan.

I was introduced to Tommy Carlin from Ivan Tors Films, the company handling the underwater photography, and we went scuba diving in the area where the Vulcan sequence was due to be filmed. I was watching the underwater filming with Tommy when

FAR LEFT: Standing in the bomb bay of the full-size Vulcan.

LEFT: The blue skies and clear waters of the Bahamas made it an ideal location.

BELOW LEFT: The full-size Vulcan on the quayside.

BELOW RIGHT: The Vulcan is lifted onto the barge.

Above left: Filming the eighth-scale Vulcan.

Above right: The quarter-size Vulcan model 'flies' at South Beach.

Far right above: John Stears and his assistant Joe Fitt, sitting on one of the scaffold towers that was built to suspend the quarter-size Vulcan.

Far right below: Jack Manson, who ran Allied Marine, loaned us this boat for use in the film.

Below: Time off at South Beach. One of Johnny Stears' towers is in the background.

Lamar Boren, the lighting cameraman, swam over to us. After grunting at me he put a couple of lead weights on my fins and passed me a bloody great lamp to help him light the set.

There were initial problems with a lack of equipment at the location, but a phone call to Charles Russhon, the film's technical advisor, got things moving. Charlie was a retired Colonel from the US Air Force and Cubby's 'fix it' man.

A barge from Miami delivered a derrick crane, which we hoped would lift the various props into the water. One day we nearly lost Ronnie Meeks, one of our riggers, when a chain holding the *Disco Volante*'s underwater compartment snapped. Ronnie jumped out of the way as the compartment dropped onto the deck. Fortunately nobody got hurt and nothing much was damaged, but the derrick crane clearly wasn't capable of lifting very heavy objects. We tried it once with the full-size Vulcan and the whole barge nearly capsized. The solution came from Harry Saltzman, who turned up at Paradise Island saying, "I hear you fellas are in trouble." He reassured us that a boat was on its way from Andros Island, with a crane that would be big enough to get everything into the water.

At South Beach Johnny Stears built two huge towers that were used to suspend the quarter-size Vulcan for its descent onto the water. With careful editing, the model was big enough to look reasonable in comparison to the size of the waves. The shots with the eighth-size model were done in a nearby reef that Johnny had found. Johnny was unwell on the day we came to shoot this, so there was only me and the cameraman underwater, in our scuba gear. Unfortunately this Vulcan didn't sink to the bottom in the way we'd intended – its aerodynamic shape gave it an unrealistic wobble that spoiled the illusion of weight. We lifted it back up and I had a hole drilled in the tail. This enabled us to attach it to a pendulum that steadily dragged it down, eventually tethering it to the sea bed.

Bill Suiter, the stuntman playing the pilot, then got into the cockpit of the full-size set, which was lowered to the sea bed. Once the set was in place we filmed the scene where the canopy detaches and he attempts to get out.

While we were working on the Vulcan, the renovated *Disco Volante* arrived at Paradise Island, complete with its cocoon. They did a beautiful job in Miami and we all agreed that this elaborate, two-part boat looked sensational.

Terence Young, the director of the film, was busy elsewhere with the actors and he wasn't present for any of our work with the Vulcan. We would see him in Nassau, however, running the film set

ABOVE LEFT AND RIGHT: The full-size Vulcan is lowered beneath the waves.

BELOW LEFT: The *Disco Volante* cocoon was constructed in Miami.

BELOW RIGHT: Fred Heyl, who captained the barge from Miami, took these pictures of the *Disco Volante*'s destruction.

Above left: Special effects assistant Michael White made many of the gadgets that Bond used in the film.

Above right: One of the boats we commandeered in the Bahamas.

Below left: My brief moment as Bond, discovering Palazzi's body in the Vulcan cockpit. This scene was filmed at Pinewood.

Below right: Moments later, Sean Connery's Bond examines Palazzi's dog tags, in a shot from the filming in the Bahamas.

in flamboyant style with Champagne, fine wines and expensive cigarettes. He'd previously behaved this way on the first two pictures, *Dr No* and *From Russia With Love*, reportedly in an effort to train Sean for the role of Bond. I could see he was trying to set an example, but I think he was also a bit of a snob who lived like Bond anyway.

Cubby was in Nassau as well. He was always a gentleman, but the location filming of *Thunderball* was the only time I ever saw him lose his temper. They needed a small boat for Domino (Claudine Auger) and the guy on the crew responsible for hiring it was moaning about the money. He kept on about it so much that one day Cubby snapped at him, "Shut up for fuck's sake and just buy the fucking thing." Cubby was that kind of person – he wanted to trust his crew and not waste time on small decisions.

Kevin McClory was quite a character. He was married to the heiress 'Bobo' Sigrist, so was already a wealthy man before he sued Bond creator Ian Fleming for the film rights to *Thunderball*. He had useful local knowledge of the Bahamas, but when he went scuba diving I remember the divers would have to follow him down to pick up all the things he dropped. One night we all went to a party at the house in Nassau once owned by the murdered entrepreneur Sir Harry Oakes. I remember Kevin and Sean had some kind of a tussle and both fell into the swimming pool. Despite this they remained quite friendly.

When the Bahamas shoot was over we returned to Pinewood and discovered that we didn't have everything we needed to complete the underwater Vulcan sequence. So we blacked out the Pinewood tank and put the adapted Valiant cockpit inside it. For one of the shots in the tank I doubled for Sean, who was busy elsewhere. So I can say with some justification that I played James Bond, albeit only in the brief scene where he removes the dog tags from Domino's brother's body. If you blink you'll miss me!

While we waited for the film to be released I expected to receive my notice, but Peter Murton told us we were all staying on for the next one. He advised me to take a holiday, and after that I was asked to make some drawings for the refurbishment of Cubby's town house in Green Street, Mayfair.

Of all the props in *Thunderball*, I think I was most complimented on the pen-like device that we made for Bond when he's trapped beneath the cover of Largo's swimming pool. Gripping the device between his teeth, he's able to get enough air to enable him to swim through an adjoining shark tunnel and out to safety. Shortly after the film's release in December 1965 I received a phone call from a representative of the Royal Engineers. "We think you've made a remarkable breakthrough," said the excited voice at the other end of the line. "It's incredible that the actor in your film can breathe underwater for so long with just this small apparatus in his mouth. How long does each one last?"

There was no way to let him down gently. "They last for as long as you can hold your breath," I said, trying to keep a straight face. "Anything longer than that is down to the editor!"

Above: A close-up of the breathing device that got the Royal Engineers so excited.

Below left: Domino (Claudine Auger) and Bond at Café Martinique in Nassau.

Below right: A souvenir from the film – one of the Café Martinique menus.

YOU ONLY LIVE TWICE

By 1966 I had settled into a pattern of either making films for Eon Productions or for its co-founder Harry Saltzman. It was fulfilling work on good-quality pictures and we felt like part of a team.

Peter Murton had accepted an offer to become the art director on the Tommy Steele musical *Half a Sixpence*, so his place on *You Only Live Twice* was taken by Harry Pottle. I'd worked with Harry many times before, mainly at Beaconsfield Studios where we'd made *Crooks Anonymous* and *The Fast Lady* in 1962. In 1963 I had been one of his assistants on the filmed television series *The Human Jungle*.

You Only Live Twice was conceived as the biggest, most outlandish Bond film to date – the aim was not only to surpass *Thunderball* but also a comedy version of Ian Fleming's *Casino Royale* that was in production at Shepperton at the same time.

Director Lewis Gilbert and production designer Ken Adam conducted their major location reconnaissance for *You Only Live Twice* in Japan, where the story was set. While flying over the island in helicopters they spotted a number of volcanoes. Shortly after they landed, Ken suggested that the villain, Blofeld (Donald Pleasence), should have a hideaway inside one of them. And so the film's most celebrated concept was born.

Ken's team in Japan included the set decorator David Ffolkes. Shooting was underway when David suddenly died from natural causes at the age of just 53. Vernon Dickson and I were promoted to take his place, but the credit on the film remained with David as a mark of respect.

While Vernon concentrated on the interior sets I was assigned to the huge volcano. In the film, the volcano is revealed to be far more sophisticated than it initially seems when a space capsule re-enters the Earth's atmosphere and descends towards it. The lake at the top literally slides away, allowing the capsule to land inside. Ken began working on the volcano designs in April, passing his sketches to Roy Dorman, the chief draughtsman. Nearly 400 drawings and three scale models would be created in preparation for the biggest interior set ever constructed in Europe.

We had originally considered building the volcano out of tubular scaffolding, but we soon realised that the structure wouldn't have anything like the strength we needed. The structural cover was instead designed by construction company Delta Doric. Bill Brown, one of

Opposite page: Tiger Tanaka's ninjas begin their assault on SPECTRE's volcano base.

Above: Lois Maxwell, Akiko Wakabayashi, Sean Connery, Karin Dor and Mie Hama on the huge volcano set at Pinewood Studios.

the company's engineers, ordered giant H irons that were 108 feet long and 33 by 12 inches. Once they were ready, Bill had to transport them from Darlington to Slough, which is Pinewood's nearest railway station. The irons arrived on the train, but they were too big to make the final part of the journey to Pinewood. Each one had to be split in half and plated back together once they reached us. It was quite a feat, but the first piece of steel finally went up on 11 May. More than 700 tons of structural steel went into the volcano, held in place by more than half a million tubular couplings. The plasterwork that went over the top was estimated to weigh around 200 tons. Once it was complete, the structure was so big that it could be seen from the London-Oxford road, three miles away.

Another unforeseen problem was blacking out the set when the sliding roof was open – we couldn't have daylight pouring in during the scenes that were supposed to be set at night. There was no way round it but to construct a huge, tubular steel rig above the set and to cover it in tarpaulin.

Circling the inner perimeter of Blofeld's base was a monorail that I predicted would be a major challenge. While flicking through a copy of the *Yellow Pages*, however, I was surprised to discover that there was a company called Monorail in Uxbridge, very near to Pinewood. I asked them for a brochure, which illustrated some of the monorails they made for delivering cement to various locations around building sites. They sent someone to Pinewood, who explained that creating a monorail for our volcano set would be easy. They were

Above left: SPECTRE personnel prepare the Soviet rocket for launch.

Above right: The helicopter arrives through the sliding roof of the volcano.

Right and far right: The monorail was a working device I sourced from a company in Uxbridge.

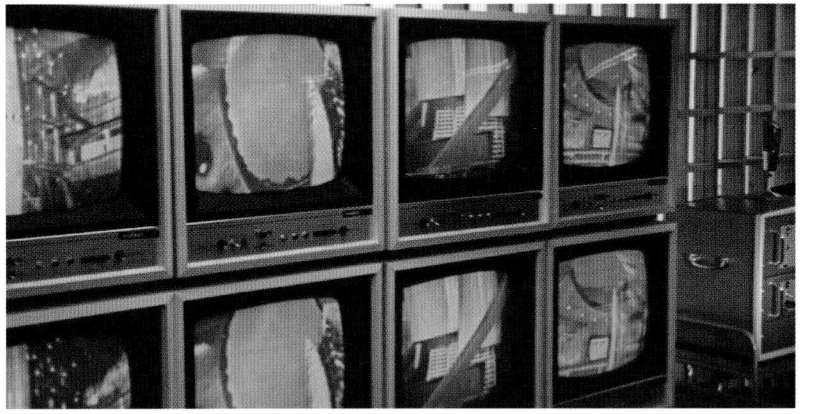

Far left: Ernst Stavro Blofeld (Donald Pleasence) in the SPECTRE control room.

Left: It was impossible to film these monitor screens until we adjusted the frame rate of the cameras.

Below right: Blofeld was originally played by Jan Werich, who is pictured here inside one of the monorail carriages in November 1966.

Below left: Filming was well underway when Werich was replaced by Pleasence.

more than happy to apply their expertise to a James Bond film, and I was extremely pleased to find such an ideal solution on our doorstep.

Some of the other challenges came from unexpected places. The SPECTRE control room inside the volcano was fitted with banks of black-and-white television monitors, all of which displayed distracting horizontal bars when we examined the rushes from the first day's filming. Televisions refresh their images at the rate of 25 frames per second, while film cameras generally shoot at 24 frames per second. The cameras had to be adjusted to shoot an extra frame per second in order the make the frame bars disappear.

Amongst my press cuttings I've got a piece from *The Sunday Times* written by the eminent critic Dilys Powell. We were all pleased that she was impressed by the sets in *You Only Live Twice*. "Ken Adam has outdone himself," she wrote. "The elegant, industrial office, Blofeld's sub-volcanic headquarters with the monorail and the camouflaged sliding roof and the rocket-launching pad – everybody concerned in the erection of the huge sets has done wonders... The machines have taken over at last."

A group of executives from our distributor, United Artists, had already expressed their admiration when they visited the set, although when one of them was told what the volcano had cost he exclaimed, "That's more than the whole of *Dr No*!"

The volcano was the centrepiece of the film, but there were many other sets and sequences to consider. The film's outstanding gadget, if that's the right word, was the single-seat autogyro that Bond uses to conduct his reconnaissance of the volcanic island. The autogyro was nicknamed Nellie and was supplied by its designer, the former RAF pilot Ken Wallis. I went up to Ken's place and surveyed the machine's various components, which in the film are delivered to Bond by Q (Desmond Llewellyn) in four large, fold-out suitcases. The suitcases were Ken's idea, and he asked for them to be covered in mock crocodile skin.

Above: Ken Wallis brings Little Nellie to Pinewood. Ken's autogyro was customised for *You Only Live Twice* by our special effects supervisor John Stears.

Right: "Now pay attention..." Q (Desmond Llewelyn) tells Bond (Sean Connery) about Little Nellie's modifications. This sequence was one of Desmond's rare trips on location.

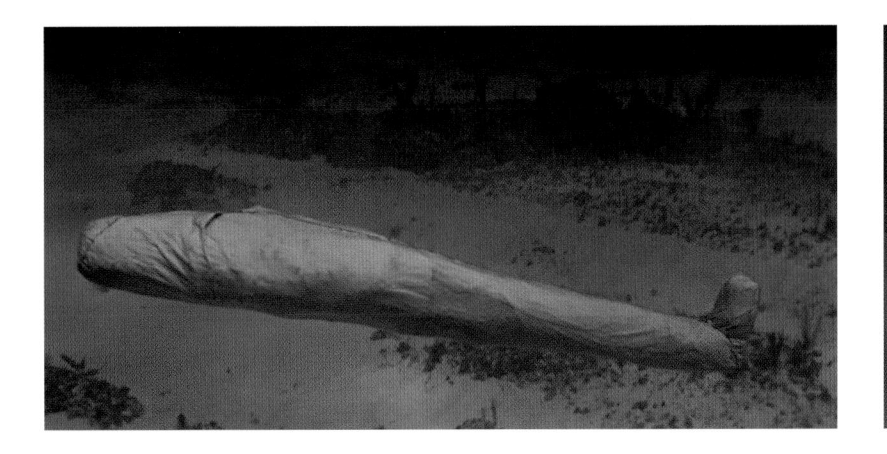

Left and far left: Bond's shroud sinks beneath the surface, before a pair of divers retrieve it from the sea bed.

Below left: The close-up of the submarine's hull, as the divers pass Bond's body through the hatch.

Below right: "Request permission to come aboard, sir." Bond arrives on the deck of the Royal Navy submarine.

Another sequence I was involved in was Bond's supposed burial at sea, staged in an effort to help convince 007's enemies that he's been murdered. Following a military funeral, Bond's body sinks to the sea bed, where it's retrieved by a pair of divers and taken to a nearby submarine. Inside the sub, Bond is cut free and emerges fresh-faced. He is immediately taken to see Moneypenny (Lois Maxwell) and M (Bernard Lee). Following his briefing he puts on a diving suit and is loaded into one of the submarine's torpedo tubes. He's fired from the submarine and swims ashore in Japan.

This section of the film comprised sequences shot on sets at Pinewood, the deck of a ship in Hong Kong, underwater in the Bahamas and a shoreline in Japan. A model submarine was built, dimly visible in the distance as the frogmen carry Bond's body away from the sea bed. We then cut to a closer shot of the submarine's hull, as the frogmen take the body into an air lock via a hatch which they close behind them. The hatch and the torpedo room were based on research I'd conducted at the Royal Navy archives, and the set was built at Pinewood's East Tunnel, which branches off E Stage.

I'd sworn I'd never go back to the Bahamas after the 14 weeks I'd spent there on *Thunderball*, but I had no choice when the crew filming the burial ran into problems. When the rushes were deemed to be unacceptable I was dispatched back to Goulding Cay, where once again I had to figure out how to make a prop sink in a convincing way. I spent about a week sweating over Bond's 'coffin', redoing it so it was negatively buoyant enough to drop to the sea bed. The coffin itself was moulded to the shape of Bond's body using chicken wire, which we then covered in linen.

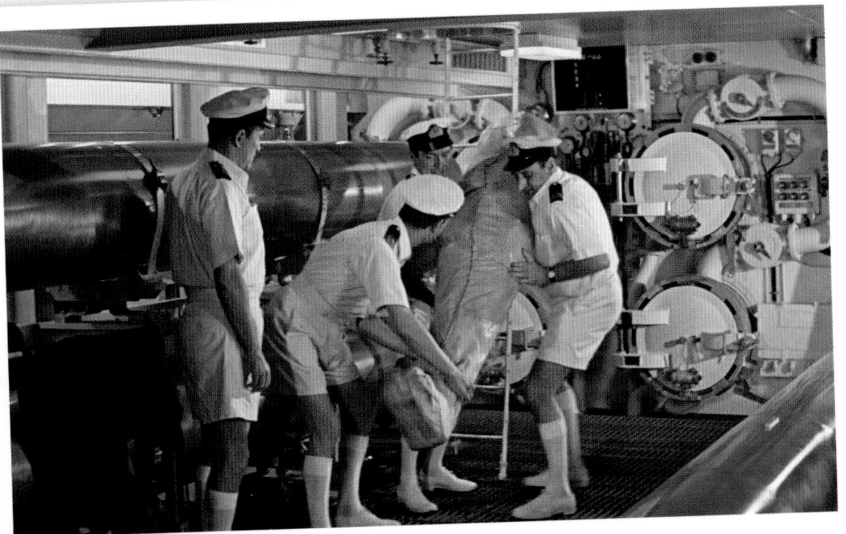

When all that was complete I figured I'd be heading home, but I received a message telling me to go to Bermuda, where Hercules planes were due to drop dinghies onto the sea in a scene from the end of the film.

There was no way to fly to Bermuda direct, so I had to go via New York. I was ill-prepared for the freezing weather that greeted me. After a quick trip to a shop in Manhattan to buy a coat I met Charlie Russhon and the crew, which included underwater cameraman Lamar Boren, who I remembered from *Thunderball*.

In Bermuda we checked in at the Castle Harbour Hotel before heading for the air base. After such a long journey it was disappointing to be told by the commanding officer that we didn't actually have permission to film the sequence. Charlie was livid, and as I

Above and far right: My six-year-old son Neil made his first contribution to the Bond films when he helped me measure up this Bell 47 helicopter.

Right: The helicopter we parked outside the interior set of Osato's penthouse suite.

accompanied him back to the hotel he said, "This is a 'Don't fuck around with Russhon' day."

Once we got to his room he put a call in to one General Short, who was the Assistant Vice-Chief of the US Air Force. "Shorty?" he said. "This is Rush. What the fuck's going on?" The next phone call was to the air base. Charlie invited the Commander, his wife and his sidekick to dinner with me and Lamar that evening. After dinner, I returned to Charlie's room with the Commander. Charlie put another call in to General Short and handed the phone to the Commander. Moments later I saw him stand to attention, and then he just kept repeating "Yes sir, yes sir, yes sir..." The General explained that everything was cleared, and the Commander then asked if he should make a report to headquarters. "Goddam it!" came the voice at the other end of the phone. "This *is* headquarters! I'm speaking to you from the Pentagon!"

The Commander wanted to be absolutely sure, however, so the following day he called the headquarters of Maritime Air Command in Orlando. He received the instruction, "Do it once, do it safely." We had three film crews covering the drops from the Hercules planes, and we got what we needed in one take.

Charlie Russhon was clearly well connected, and the co-operation of the US Air Force was a special privilege that we were careful not to advertise. For this reason, among the crew only myself, Lamar and Charlie knew that we were shooting a sequence for a James Bond film. Some of the cameramen were understandably curious about what they were filming. One of them, Dick Kratina, kept asking me, "What's a limey doing out here?" I had to tell him something, so I said, "We're making a documentary for the BBC." I could see he didn't quite believe me. "Are you sure?" he said. "Yes, of course." I replied. "Why else would I be here?"

Years later, I was reunited with Dick in New York when he joined us as a standby cameraman on *Live and Let Die*. He immediately reminded me about Bermuda. "I *knew* you were up to something that day!" he said, smiling.

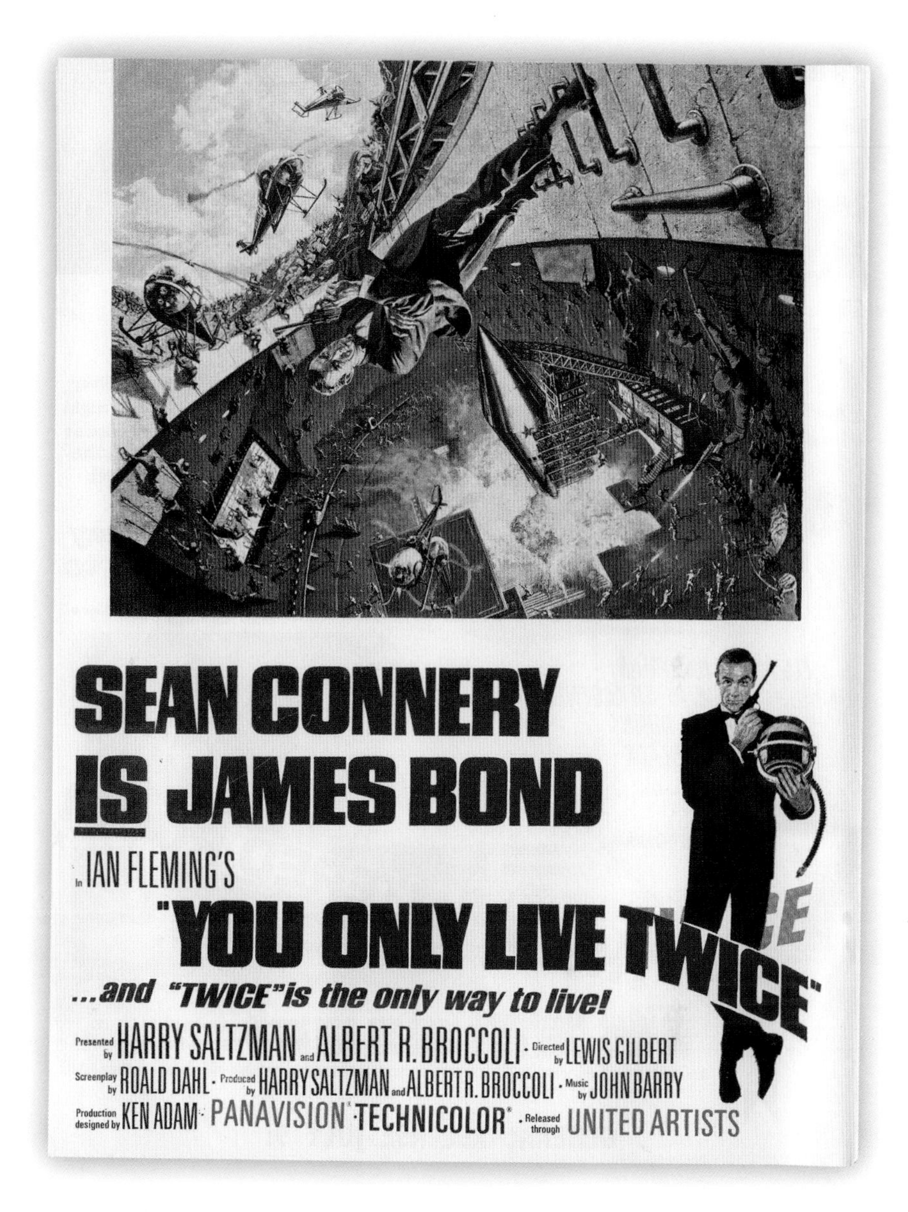

ABOVE: The volcano featured prominently in the film's advertising.

FAR LEFT: We shot this scene of the Hercules planes dropping their dinghies in one take.

LEFT: There was more time to film the rest of the sequence, as Bond and his allies scrambled onto the boats.

ON HER MAJESTY'S SECRET SERVICE

Sean Connery was already growing impatient with the demands of the James Bond films when some difficult experiences during the making of *You Only Live Twice* strengthened his resolve to quit. I was rather closer to events in the Eon art department, and there was a change at the top there too. After *Chitty Chitty Bang Bang* Ken Adam stepped aside to work on the remake of *Goodbye, Mr Chips*. The next James Bond film would have a new leading man in George Lazenby and a new director in Peter Hunt. Syd Cain was back as production designer for the first time since *From Russia With Love*.

Both Peter and Syd had been with the Bond films in different capacities since *Dr No*, but George was a novice in every respect; a former model whose first screen role was as leading man in a blockbuster movie. I remember seeing his screen test, and despite his inexperience there was no doubt in my mind that he was by far the best candidate on offer.

Pre-production of *On Her Majesty's Secret Service* began in 1968. Key to my role as the set decorator was the choice to move away from the style of bespoke centrepiece constructed for *You Only Live Twice* in favour of a spectacular real-life location. Syd and Harry Saltzman had already considered, and dismissed, several places before they followed a recommendation by Hubert Fröhlich, the film's location manager, and visited the site of a proposed restaurant on the summit of the Schilthorn mountain in Switzerland. It was easy to see why Syd and Harry were so impressed – the Schilthornbahn had been under construction since 1961 and still wasn't finished, but the circular design of its Alpine Room offered a spectacular,

OPPOSITE PAGE: Bond (George Lazenby) and Ruby Bartlett (Angela Scoular) at Piz Gloria. We fitted special filters to the windows to balance the sunset with the interior lights.

ABOVE LEFT: Filming in the Alpine Room. I'm standing far left, dressed in black.

ABOVE RIGHT: The cable car approaches Piz Gloria from the mid-station on the Schilthorn.

RIGHT AND BELOW: Views of Piz Gloria from the cable car, showing some of the construction work we undertook in 1968.

BELOW RIGHT: The underside of the cable car that took us to and from the location every day.

360-degree view that took in the Eiger, Mönch and Jungfrau mountains, along with some 200 other peaks. The village of Mürren was at the foot of the mountain, and other locations were found at the nearby Lauterbrunnen and Grindelwald. It all added up to the kind of package that just couldn't be recreated at Pinewood.

Syd would order 500 tons of concrete to be hauled to the Schilthorn, constructing a helicopter pad, completing a lot of the unfinished interior work in the restaurant and installing a new 2,000-amp generator to help power the camera crew's lights. The helipad and the restaurant renovations are still there. Another legacy of the film's production is the name Piz Gloria, which was taken from Ian Fleming's original novel and has been adopted by the restaurant ever since. The final bill for adapting the Schilthornbahn came to $60,000 – a lot of money by anyone's standards in 1968, but a bargain compared to what had been spent on Pinewood's volcano set for *You Only Live Twice*.

On my first reconnaissance to the Schilthornbahn I was accompanied by Syd and art director Robert Laing. I was overwhelmed – I had never seen a place like it – but my thoughts soon turned to the practicalities. We were going to shoot a lot of interiors inside the building and everything needed dressing. In autumn 1968 Bob and I would go to Switzerland every week, staying at a very nice hotel right by the train station in Mürren and striking up relationships with the locals who might be able to help us.

Piz Gloria needed a well-stocked bar, and following an agreement to feature Teacher's whisky in the film we received 300 bottles. I was at the mid-station, half way between Mürren and the summit of the Schilthorn, when I first met J Bartlett Morgan, the Canadian who part-owned the Schilthornbahn. Bartlett was essentially our landlord, and it was perhaps out of deference that everyone on the crew addressed him as 'Mr Morgan'. He was a lovely man who took a close interest in all the activity taking place up and down the mountain. He told me he'd heard that we'd done a deal with Teacher's for the whisky – would we also like some gin? He was friendly with Alan Burrough, who ran the company that owned the Beefeater brand. Before we knew it, 300 bottles of Beefeater gin arrived at Mürren Station. The next time I bumped into Mr Morgan I said, "Of course, one drink we really need for a James Bond film is Dom Perignon Champagne..." He quite casually said, "Oh, I know them too." Three weeks later four cases of the stuff turned up.

Top left: Meeting some of the wildlife in Mürren.

Top right: The chalet where I stayed with assistant art director Robert Laing.

Above: The view of the Eiger, Mönch and Jungfrau mountains from the summit of the Schilthorn.

Left: George Lazenby relaxes with the girls playing the Angels of Death during a break in filming at Piz Gloria.

ABOVE LEFT: Bond and Blofeld's girls at Piz Gloria. This is another example of how the filters on the windows of the Alpine Room balanced the light.

ABOVE RIGHT: Director of photography Michael Reed (left) and camera operator Alec Mills (centre) outside Piz Gloria.

The Alpine Room was surrounded by 24 windows, each measuring six by eight feet. These weren't props, but a problem with the lighting meant that adapting them became my responsibility. Michael Reed, our director of photography, told me that all the glass would need special filters so he'd be able to clearly show the view outside without the light flaring. We decided to cover the windows with acrylic Plexiglass, each piece cut to the exact size and dyed with the necessary filters in the Pinewood prop department. I went to see Bert Driscoll, who was the head of prop-making. He said he'd be happy to help but pointed out that his tank was only three by three feet. The solution, I decided, was to build him a bigger tank. Once this was ready, each pane of Plexiglass was dyed with a combination of up to three dyes, individually boxed and sent to Switzerland. Bert spent four weeks toiling over his new tank, with various shades of coloured steam rising in plumes around his ears. Mike said he looked like one of the witches from *Macbeth*.

When the set dressing of Piz Gloria was complete, Peter Hunt arrived in Mürren to begin shooting. Peter was an outstanding editor who had helped to create the style of the Bond films. He was also the sort of director you felt you could talk to at any time. I said to him, "Peter, I think you should come with me to Piz Gloria. Once all the lights and cameras are in you'll never see it looking like this again." When we arrived at the top of the mountain Peter was delighted with what he saw. "I think we should celebrate!" he announced, so Syd and I opened some bottles of Champagne. Syd didn't drink, so just touched the glass to his lips and said, "This is really nice." Peter tried some of his, screwed his face up and said, "It's bloody ginger ale!" Ronnie Quelch, the production buyer, had also ordered bottles of dummy Champagne which we'd opened by mistake.

FAR LEFT AND LEFT: The girls receive their deadly parting gifts from Blofeld. These vanity cases were specially made for us by Asprey of New Bond Street.

BELOW: A stunning view of Piz Gloria showing the lack of snow in late 1968.

Much of the film's action on location required thick snow, and we'd been assured that this would start falling at the beginning of October. The date came and went and the weather remained stubbornly mild. In Switzerland everything closed at noon on Saturdays so we worked all weekend and had Fridays off. As luck would have it, the snow finally arrived on a Thursday night, so all leave was hastily rearranged. Hubert had hired six Italian labourers to build the helipad, but on Friday morning they were given shovels and told to pile the snow up at strategic points to make it appear thicker than it actually was. I'd never seen anyone work so fast.

There were interiors to prepare at Pinewood, but I stayed in Mürren for some of the location shooting and was on hand to deliver the vanity cases that Blofeld (Telly Savalas) gave to each of his Angels of Death, the beautiful patients at his so-called allergy clinic. The atomisers in these cases would launch Blofeld's deadly bacteria when the girls returned to the outside world. Ronnie knew John Asprey of the famous Asprey jewellers. In fact he was one of the few buyers who could get Asprey to hire any of their products for use in a film. Ronnie took me to the shop in New Bond Street, where John showed us the company's vanity cases. We took one back to show Peter Hunt, who admired the craftsmanship but said it was too big. John then said that if we supplied the materials he would make a box to our specifications. Valley Tools, a company in Uxbridge, then made most of the accoutrements inside.

There was one case for each of the girls, and each case was gift-wrapped with paper and ribbon that also came from Asprey. Unfortunately Peter shot the unwrapping scene something like five times, so before each take we had to quickly rewrap the things as we had no spares. The girls included Jenny Hanley, Joanna Lumley and Catherine Schell. They were all very friendly, and because there wasn't much to do in Mürren we'd often invite them to our chalets for drinks and dinner.

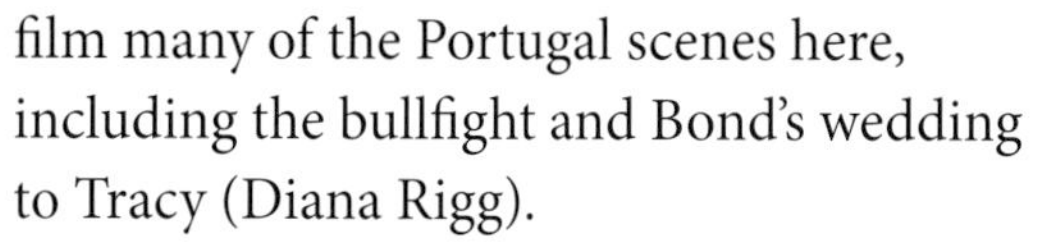

Above left: The four stooges – production buyer Ronnie Quelch, chief draughtsman Roy Dorman, myself and construction manager Ronnie Udell, having dinner at a restaurant in Portugal.

Above right: Mr and Mrs Bond look forward to their honeymoon.

Below left: The bullring at Herdade do Zambujal, as it appeared in the film.

Below right: A picture from my reconnaissance, showing the location before it was dressed.

At the end of 1968 I went home for Christmas. Work on the film resumed in January, and while Peter Hunt was still filming in Switzerland I went to Portugal with Roy Dorman, Ronnie Quelch and the construction manager Ronnie Udell. The first location we visited was one of the most important. Herdade do Zambujal is a large, medieval estate near Setúbal. Generations have lived their entire lives on this estate and the current owners, the Vinhas family, were happy for us to film many of the Portugal scenes here, including the bullfight and Bond's wedding to Tracy (Diana Rigg).

We were introduced to Fernando Pessa, a local television personality who – like Charlie Russhon in the US – seemed to be very well connected and could get you in anywhere you wanted to go. There had recently been a big society wedding in Lisbon, so we hired the same caterer. He then put us in touch with the florist he had worked with, a guy called Romero who festooned the place. I'd never seen so many flowers in my life – it looked beautiful. When they wilted after a rain shower they were all replaced within 50 minutes.

We all stayed in the same hotel and on the first night Bernard Lee (who once again played M) got drunk and played the piano. I remember he tore his trousers during filming of the wedding.

We used some of Romero's flowers to decorate the car that Bond and Tracy use to drive away on their honeymoon. This was the car that Tracy

LEFT: Three views of Herdade do Zambujal from my reconnaissance trip. The estate is vast and offered us a number of possibilities for different settings.

BELOW: George Lazenby (as Bond) and Diana Rigg (as Tracy) during filming at Pinewood. I wasn't quite so reckless when I visited a real casino in Portugal.

was in when Irma Bunt (Ilse Steppat) assassinated her at the end of the film. The end credits play over an image of the shattered windscreen, but I painted the damage onto the glass – we never actually made a hole in it.

While we were shooting in Portugal, Syd, Roy, Ronnie Quelch and myself went to a casino. We were doing quite well in our own modest way when Cubby arrived and told us we should be more adventurous. He took all our chips and put them on number 36. Soon after the roulette wheel stopped spinning we realised we'd lost the lot. No problem for Cubby, who turned to Stanley Sopel, the associate producer, and asked for some more money. This time he put everything on number 11. It came up, and suddenly there was a mountain of plaques on our table. He gave us a heap of chips and said, "That's how you do it. There are four tables here – play then all simultaneously." And with that he and Stanley walked away. Cubby always liked to see the boys on his crew enjoying themselves.

The film wrapped in June 1969, by which time George Lazenby had told Cubby and Harry that he would never do another Bond picture. Diana Rigg had lost patience with George's behaviour during the filming and she wasn't the only one who had reservations about him. Richard Maibaum, the film's screenwriter, visited us in Portugal and told me, "If Sean had been in this it would have been great." Peter Hunt had championed George the previous year, but shortly after the film was delivered he told me, "My only mistake was not revoicing him for the whole thing."

George's decision to quit may have contributed to some of the hostile reviews his performance received when the film opened in December. I know George has long since realised that he should have stayed with James Bond longer, but I hope he's proud of the film we made. Whatever issues may have existed at the time, I think *On Her Majesty's Secret Service* has aged well.

DIAMONDS ARE FOREVER

Quite a lot of uncertainly surrounded the next James Bond film, *Diamonds Are Forever*, beginning with the identity of the leading man. It's been well-documented that Sean Connery was eventually persuaded to return to the role – supposedly for the final time – by a seven-figure salary that he donated to the Scottish International Education Trust. Once this was resolved questions remained about where the film would be shot.

In early 1971 I returned home from working on *Fiddler on the Roof* to find a message saying that Stanley Sopel wanted to meet me at Pinewood. I had understood that *Diamonds Are Forever* would be produced in the United States and was aware that space had already been booked at Universal Studios in Los Angeles. Stanley explained that whatever tax considerations had prompted Eon to shift production out of the UK no longer applied; the locations would largely be shot in America, but the studio work would once again be based at Pinewood. Ken Adam was returning as production designer and Jack Maxsted would be the UK art director. He needed a UK set decorator and he offered me the job. I accepted on the condition that I could also work on the American part of the shoot.

I had an American counterpart in John Austin, but I still spent quite a lot of time in the States, most memorably in Las Vegas. As the plane approached I looked out of the window and saw the town in the distance, lit up like a shining diamond in the desert. I checked in to the Riviera, a huge high-rise hotel and casino on the Las Vegas Strip, and met Ken. I don't know who owned the hotel at the time, but I think Cubby had pulled some strings because we all stayed there for free. The casinos and shows felt like another world, somehow detached from reality – with no windows and no clocks, you could gamble for hours and begin to lose a sense of when the night ended and the next day began.

OPPOSITE PAGE: Harry Saltzman, Albert 'Cubby' Broccoli and director Guy Hamilton on the moonscape set at Pinewood.

ABOVE LEFT: Ken Adam was born in Berlin, and we affectionately referred to him as 'The Red Baron'.

ABOVE RIGHT: Sean Connery and Cubby on set. This would be their last film together.

Right and far right: Bond's Mustang Mach 1 evades the police on the streets of Las Vegas. When we got back to Pinewood we had to film an extra scene to correct the continuity, as the car appeared to emerge from the other end of the alleyway on the wrong set of wheels!

Right centre: Leroy Hollis as the Las Vegas Sheriff. Leroy was also our transportation manager.

Below: Harry Saltzman at Pinewood in 1971.

As well as filming inside the Riviera, a lot of work was done on the streets outside. Howard Hughes, the reclusive billionaire who owned so much of the town, had offered Cubby whatever facilities the film needed. This extended to closing off the strip to allow director Guy Hamilton to film the Sheriff (Leroy Hollis) and his traffic cops pursuing Bond and Tiffany Case (Jill St John) on an extended chase that ended with Bond tipping his Mustang onto two wheels to squeeze it through a tight alleyway.

The chase was filmed at night, and I vividly remember standing outside the Golden Nugget casino as the cars tore past us. "Where are your lights?" Harry Saltzman asked Ted Moore, the director of photography. Ted got his light meter out and showed it to Harry. "Look," he said. "I don't need any!" The Strip was bathed in so much artificial light from the glittering facades of the hotels and casinos that, even in the pitch dark of the Nevada evening, the sequence lit itself.

The car chase is one of the film's highlights, but it caused a few headaches for our associate producer Stanley Sopel. Poor old Stanley had to keep finding more cars so continuity could be maintained throughout the shoot. The whole thing was such a wreckers' derby that he ended up buying 55.

The scenes with Tiffany at Circus Circus – a hotel with the world's largest permanent big top – meant that I needed to pay close attention to the sideshows as well as the acrobats. 'Zambora', the caged woman who apparently transforms into a 450-pound gorilla in front of an audience of children, was based on a trick I actually witnessed. I found out how it was done, and we replicated the illusion at Pinewood using the same system of mirrors.

Bond gains access to the penthouse suite where Blofeld (Charles Gray) is lurking by casually hitching a lift on top of an elevator that ascends the outside of his hotel. These scenes were originally filmed at the Landmark, a mushroom-shaped hotel that had been opened by Howard Hughes in 1969, but they were supplemented with material we shot at Pinewood later. One of the problems with the location footage was that the film wasn't fast enough to capture the detail of the lights, buildings and cars in the Strip below the lift, and Guy felt there wasn't a sufficient sense that Bond was risking his life so high above the ground. So we built a prop lift at Pinewood and my brother Michael, along with the chief electrician Johnny Dyke, built a miniature version of the Strip with moving lights to represent the cars and so on. It can be seen in the sequence where Bond fires the pitons into the overhanging concrete and climbs onto the roof.

The exterior of the Slumber Inc mortuary was on an old highway several miles outside Las Vegas. The exterior of the building had a distinctive window in the

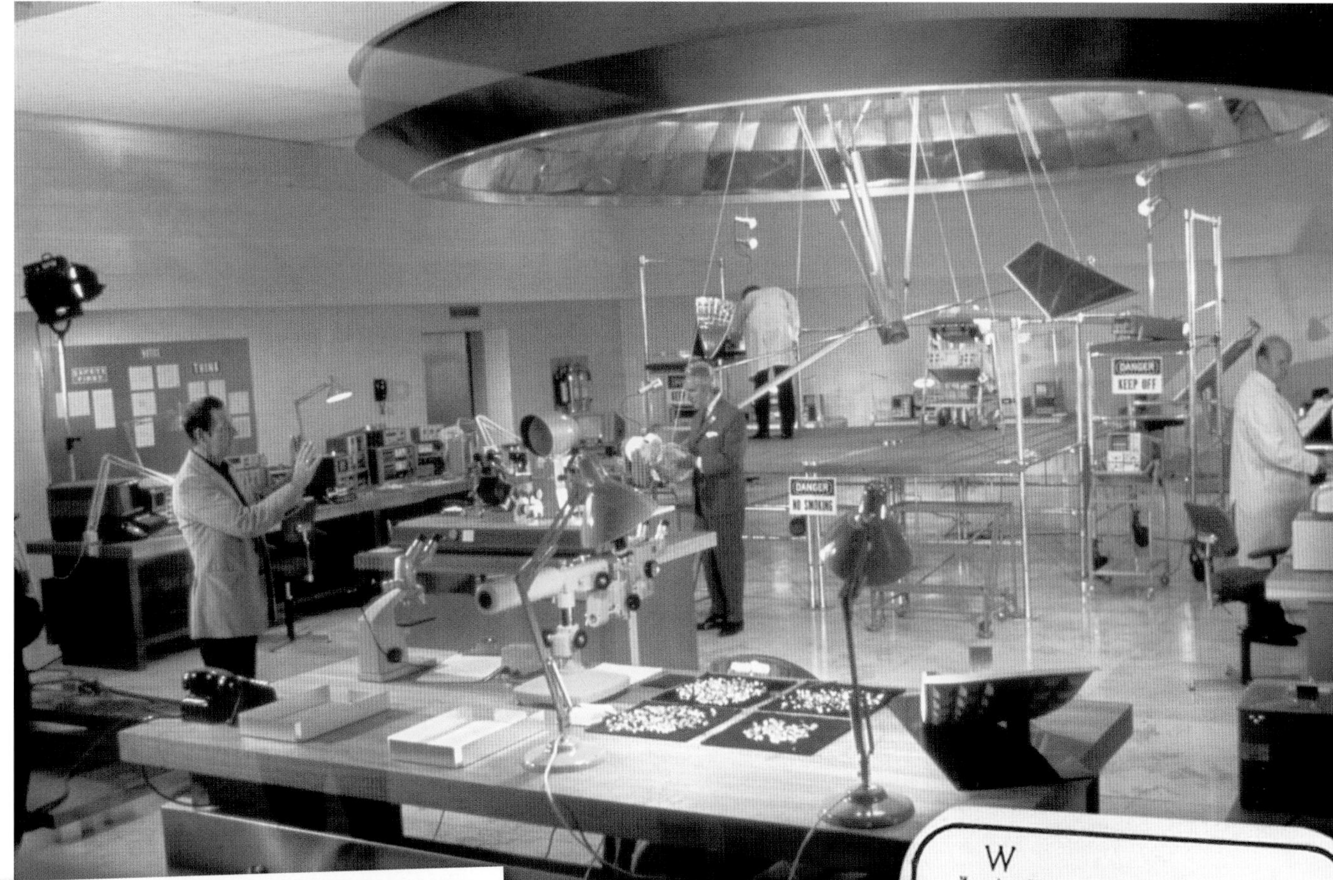

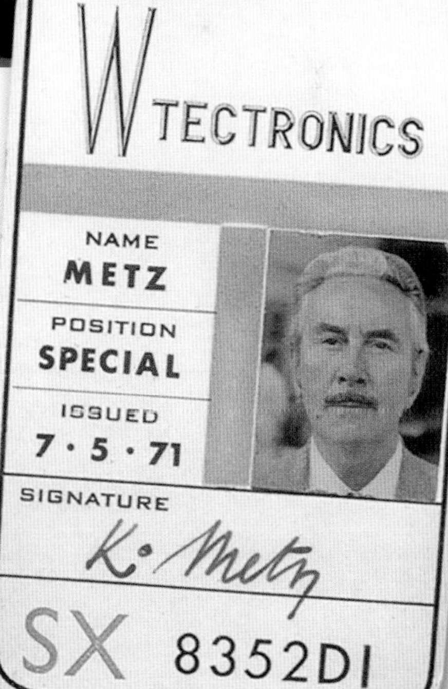

Above: Guy Hamilton (left) with Joseph Fürst (as Dr Metz, centre) in the satellite laboratory, one of the sets I dressed at Pinewood.

Right: The security pass I made for Joseph's character, Dr Metz.

Left: Bond fires pitons to gain entry to Blofeld's penthouse suite. The view behind him was an elaborate model built by my brother, Michael, and John Dyke.

Below left: Bond meets Blofeld (Charles Gray), or rather several Blofelds, in the penthouse. I still have one of the lights hanging over the desk.

Below right: Bond in the lift that I decorated with steel tiles from Germany.

shape of an upturned diamond. We were going to build the interior at Pinewood, but Ken asked me to have a look inside the real place anyway, in case it offered any inspiration. I walked through the door to see a Native American family gathered round an open coffin. I paused, but then one of the staff ordered them to "Get back – it's a fella from the films and he wants to take some pictures." Before I could say anything they had already started moving away. I felt so embarrassed.

The filming at Pinewood began on A Stage in June 1971 with the scenes in Blofeld's penthouse suite. Ken's set made no attempt to rival the extravagance of *You Only Live Twice* or the natural splendour of *On Her Majesty's Secret Service*, but still bore many of his elegant trademarks. Blofeld's desk was lit by a pair of Arco floor lamps, based on a classic Italian design from the early 1960s. I don't have to look far to be reminded of this film, because when production was complete I bought one of the lamps and took it home. It's still in my living room.

After his initial confrontation with Blofeld, Bond gets into the elevator and presses the button that he expects will take him to the lobby. He is on the way down when gas leaking from the ceiling knocks him unconscious. I got hold of some distinctive tiles to decorate the interior of the lift. They were made of stainless steel and I ordered them specially from a company in West Germany. It wasn't easy getting them to Pinewood, but I think it was worth it.

Several weekend locations took us to Cannes and Frankfurt while filming continued at Pinewood during the week. On another weekend I flew out to Amsterdam, where the next stage of location filming was due to take place. Along with the stills man George Whitear and the continuity girl Elaine Schreyeck we visited the spot where the elderly Mrs Whistler (Margaret Lacey) was due to be dragged from the water. We were on the canal when we spotted a sex shop on a street corner, so at lunchtime we decided to have a look inside. The woman sitting behind the counter was wearing a baby-doll nightie. After a few minutes she said, "Are you buying?" We explained that we were just looking. She glared at us. "If you're not buying you can fuck off!"

There was a slightly warmer reception at Dover, where Bond receives his fake passport from Miss Moneypenny (Lois Maxwell). I remember the Triumph Stag driven by Bond in those scenes was one of a handful of prototypes of a car that had yet to reach the market. In fact ours was number seven.

Although Guy Hamilton had previously directed *Goldfinger*, I got to know him much better during *Diamonds Are Forever*. Guy was extremely calm, never raised his voice, and brought filming to an end bang on schedule. He paid me a great compliment when he said, "You know Peter, if I ask you to do something you always give me what I need." All these years later, I can't think of a better way to sum up my attitude to Guy and all the other directors I worked with at that time.

Above left: Bond avoids a premature cremation at Slumber Inc. This picture was taken in August 1971, on Sean's penultimate day.

Above right: A publicity shot of Sean and his co-star Jill St John.

Far left: Mrs Whistler's body is dragged from the canal in Amsterdam.

Left: The prototype Triumph Stag arrives at Dover.

EVINRUDE
10
SHERIFF'S
DEPARTMENT

LIVE AND LET DIE

Guy Hamilton lent some continuity to proceedings by signing on to direct *Live and Let Die*. It was some time later that the film's lead role was taken by Roger Moore, the charismatic star who would provide some much-needed staying power in the role of James Bond.

Syd Cain was the supervising art director (in those days the choice between this and the title 'production designer' was a matter of personal preference) and he offered me a promotion from set decorator to co-art director, alongside Robert Laing. Work was well underway when I started in spring 1972 – Syd and Guy had recently returned from Jamaica and Bob was still out there. For the next reconnaissance I joined Harry Saltzman, Guy and Syd on a visit to New Orleans. These trips were made in advance of Tom Mankiewicz completing his final draft of the screenplay; we were looking for suitable places to film and also coming up with suggestions that might influence the action.

The first leg of the journey took us to New York. "I like to look after my boys," said Harry, so we flew first class. During the flight we joined Harry for a meal in the dining section. We were looking forward to something to eat when Harry asked the air stewardess if she could retrieve part of his hand luggage. He opened the bag to reveal what looked like a large salad. As he offered me a tomato I thought, "Blimey, he's travelling first class and he's brought his own food!" Harry explained that he had a large garden at his place in the country and was trying to live off the fruit of the land.

Our first task was to find the locations for the epic powerboat chase across the Louisiana bayou. Or rather, relocate them – we were now into early summer and many of the areas Syd and Guy had earmarked on a previous trip had become so overgrown they looked completely different. Guy introduced me to Steve Hendrickson, an art director from New

Opposite page: Sheriff JW Pepper (Clifton James) can't believe his eyes as Bond's powerboat flies over a levee in New Orleans. The audience was similarly stunned.

Above left: "What the hell am I doing here?" Shooting in New Orleans put me in a number of tricky situations.

Above right: Roger Moore strikes a confident pose, on location for his first Bond film.

Above: I took these pictures of the shipyard in Slidell, Louisiana, during our reconnaissance of the area.

Below left: Three shots of the canals near the jump site, taken from our helicopter.

Below right: Special effects supervisor Derek Meddings, on location in New Orleans. This was Derek's first Bond film, following years of pioneering work creating and filming miniatures for producer Gerry Anderson.

York, and asked us to find some interesting spots using a helicopter. We spent two weeks looking for the places in Syd and Guy's photographs, identifying new locations along the way.

On his previous visit Guy had noticed two strange-looking lagoons, and he asked us to find out how we could enter the area for the purposes of filming. Several days later I told Guy we'd found the canal that led to the lagoons and offered to take him there. Stunt driver Jerry Comeaux, special effects supervisor Derek Meddings, Guy and I climbed into a pump boat and headed for the place we'd noted on the map. When we got to there, Jerry did a huge turn and we roared across the lagoon for about half a mile before coming to a shuddering halt. Jerry jumped off the side to examine the engine, which he thought might have been clogged by debris. It turned out the engine was clear, but we'd got stuck in thick mud. Guy said, "So how the hell do we get back?" Jerry looked at him and replied, "We walk."

Guy jumped over the side of the boat, followed by Derek. I was next, but when I found myself up to my chest in mud I clambered back and adopted a new strategy. First I took my shoes off and hung them round my neck. Next I took my hat off, put my camera on top of my head and replaced my hat. Then I jumped back in. With great difficulty we waded back towards the entrance of the lagoon.

Along the way we passed a number of little islands of dead foliage. I made some inane remark about one of them probably being an alligators' nest and Jerry said, "Don't joke – you could be right!" Fortunately we didn't see any alligators, or any of the venomous cottonmouth snakes that also lived in these shallow waters.

"Right, now what?" said Guy, when we reached the entrance to the lagoon. Jerry told us to wait for him while he swam across the canal and across another lagoon to fetch his brother. While we waited, Guy asked Derek for a cigarette and wondered whether we'd have got stuck if Jerry hadn't driven into the lagoon so quickly.

Jerry eventually returned and his brother took us all back to the French Quarter Inn, where Guy was staying. The concierge gave us a very funny look as we trudged into reception, caked in mud. I never did succeed in getting my clothes clean. The following morning a helicopter flew out to the lagoon and retrieved the boat.

Guy also wanted us to find vantage points for the cameras filming the chase, and we nearly came a cropper there as well. Spotting a suitable-looking house we decided to knock on the door to introduce ourselves to the owner. I heard footsteps coming down the hallway before the letterbox opened. A double-barrelled

BELOW LEFT: An aerial view of the Slidell shipyard.

BELOW RIGHT: A list of the boats we used during the lengthy chase sequence.

BOTTOM RIGHT: I drew this sketch to illustrate the course of the boat chase.

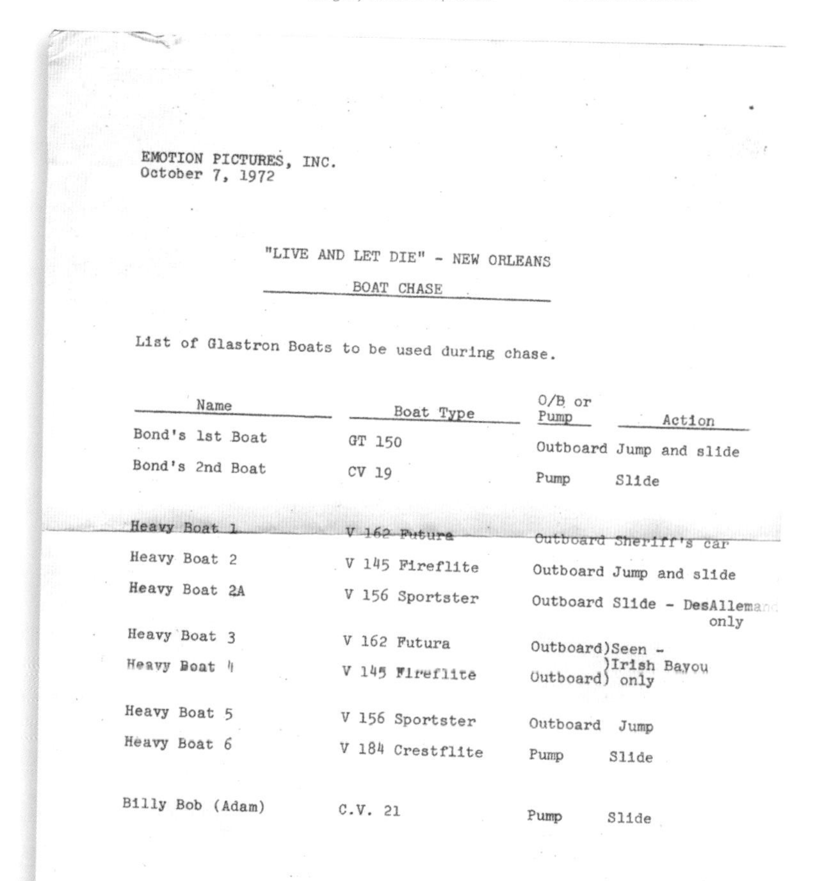

EMOTION PICTURES, INC.
October 7, 1972

"LIVE AND LET DIE" - NEW ORLEANS

BOAT CHASE

List of Glastron Boats to be used during chase.

Name	Boat Type	O/B or Pump	Action
Bond's 1st Boat	GT 150	Outboard	Jump and slide
Bond's 2nd Boat	CV 19	Pump	Slide
Heavy Boat 1	V 162 Futura	Outboard	Sheriff's car
Heavy Boat 2	V 145 Fireflite	Outboard	Jump and slide
Heavy Boat 2A	V 156 Sportster	Outboard	Slide - DesAlleman only
Heavy Boat 3	V 162 Futura	Outboard)	Seen -)Irish Bayou
Heavy Boat 4	V 145 Fireflite	Outboard)	only
Heavy Boat 5	V 156 Sportster	Outboard	Jump
Heavy Boat 6	V 184 Crestflite	Pump	Slide
Billy Bob (Adam)	C.V. 21	Pump	Slide

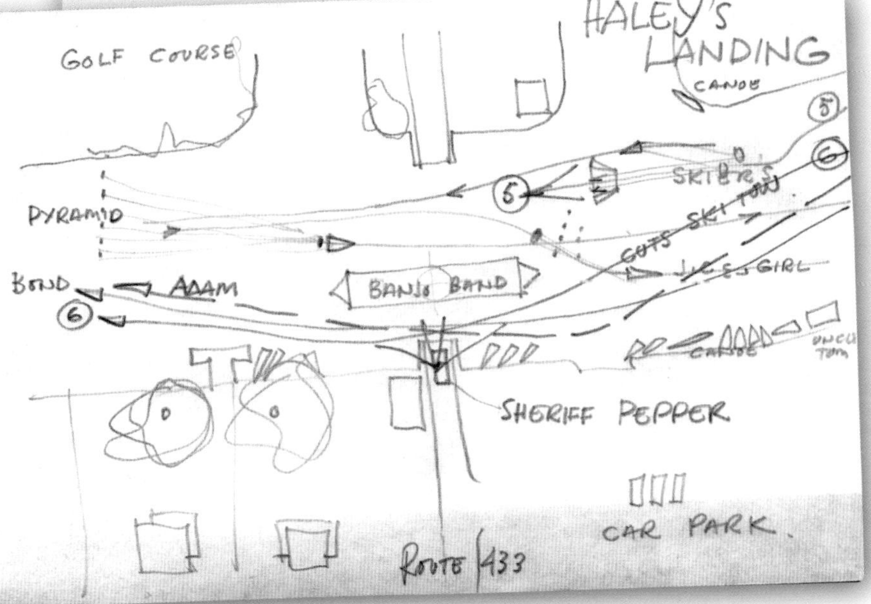

TOP: Derek pictured at the peninsula on the Treadway Estate, where the wedding sequence was filmed.

ABOVE: We needed to find an estate with a swimming pool, and this one was ideal.

RIGHT: Another aerial shot from the two-week recce I conducted with US art director Steve Hendrickson.

shotgun poked through the gap and a voice from within shouted, "Fuck off!" So we did.

We were more successful finding the peninsula where Bond's boat comes off the water and tears past a wedding party. When we landed our helicopter at the location we were met by its owners, Bill and Flo Treadway, both of whom were very helpful. They were intrigued to hear that we were scouting for a James Bond film and their young sons were particularly excited.

A few days later we were returning by boat when we were met by another local couple, Peter and Gardner Schneider, who had heard about our visit to the Treadways. Pete owned the St Joe Brick Works, a long-established business north of New Orleans, and was convalescing after a recent heart attack. Gardner was a lovely lady who seemed to know everybody in the vicinity and became our unofficial location manager for the duration of our stay.

Gardner asked what we were looking for and I told her about the part of the story where Bond's outboard motor runs out of fuel and the guy chasing him gets his boat stuck in a swimming pool. Bond then

did a bit of free renovation work. So we mowed the grass and poured a huge amount of acid into the overgrown pool, removing all the snakes and sprucing it up.

Pete and Gardner's kindness continued beyond our reconnaissance and well into the shoot, which began in October 1972. They invited us to their house for dinner every weekend, and after a while I insisted we take *them* out to dinner to show our appreciation. They suggested a restaurant called the Elmwood Plantation on River Road, so one Saturday evening a group of us, including Derek and his wife Alex, all went along.

Pete was a wine connoisseur with a well-stocked cellar, and the wine at the restaurant was clearly top notch – some of it was priced at $1,000 a bottle. As the waiter poured it into the biggest glasses I'd ever seen I started worrying about how I would justify this expense to the production accountant. When the bill arrived I noticed the wine hadn't been included. "I think you've forgotten the wine," I said to the waiter. "Not at all sir," he replied, explaining that they were so pleased to see Mr Schneider fit and well again that the wine was a gift. I handed over my American Express card with a huge sense of relief, and after that we all went to New Orleans' Bourbon Street for the live jazz.

The biggest challenge in the bayou chase was the sequence where Bond's boat launches itself up a levee, flies over the head of Sheriff JW Pepper steals another boat to make his getaway. We had found what we thought was the ideal place to shoot this sequence, only to discover that someone had recently been murdered there so the Louisiana police wouldn't allow any filming.

Gardner told us about an estate agent who was representing a run-down property with a swimming pool that backed onto the bayou. This was a good alternative, and the agent allowed us to use the pool and land on the condition that we

LEFT: Derek and supervising art director Syd Cain (centre) in New Orleans. Syd had previously run the art departments on *From Russia With Love* and *On Her Majesty's Secret Service*.

BELOW LEFT AND CENTRE: Stunt driver Jerry Comeaux rehearses the powerboat jump at New Orleans City Park.

BELOW RIGHT: Steve Hendrickson looms large in this contact sheet of photos from the jump rehearsal.

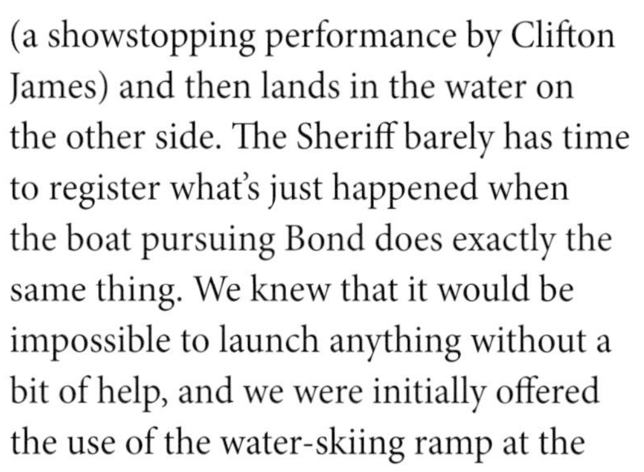

(a showstopping performance by Clifton James) and then lands in the water on the other side. The Sheriff barely has time to register what's just happened when the boat pursuing Bond does exactly the same thing. We knew that it would be impossible to launch anything without a bit of help, and we were initially offered the use of the water-skiing ramp at the New Orleans City Park. It was too short, however, and certainly wasn't strong enough to bear the weight of one boat after another. We decided to build a ramp from scratch out of steel, adding empty 50-gallon drums underneath so we could float it into position behind tall reeds that would disguise it on screen. Along the centre of the ramp's surface we fitted heavy-duty warehouse rollers that would reduce the friction on the underside of each boat. They made a hell of a clattering noise, but that didn't need to appear on the soundtrack.

Above left: Leaning against the jump ramp, with the ramp's designer – a guy called Al who owned a local boatyard.

Above right: Crew members gather on the levee to watch the filming of the second boat jump.

Right and far right: Bond's Glastron GT-150 boat speeds towards the bank of the levee.

Jerry Comeaux was doubling for Roger Moore during the chase and he met us at City Park for a rehearsal with the new ramp. The ramp was the right length, but Jerry said the boat wouldn't be able to reach the speed necessary to make the jump. The boat had an Evinrude engine, but Jerry suggested replacing it with a more powerful Mercury 125. It was only after we tried using a Mercury that Evinrude, who had a deal with the producers, decided to send us some bigger engines and an engineer to fit them.

We moved the ramp to the bank of the Harlem Back Levee Drop and filmed the jump on 16 October. Jerry did it in one take, bringing the boat to a speed of 75 miles per hour before launching it. His 110-feet jump unintentionally set a new world record. He then dressed up as Bond's pursuer and did it all over again in a boat powered by the other Evinrude engine.

For the filming of the wedding sequence on the Treadway Estate we created a makeshift ramp by shovelling some of the bank away. There were no wheels underneath Bond's boat or the one that followed it, which crashes into the wedding

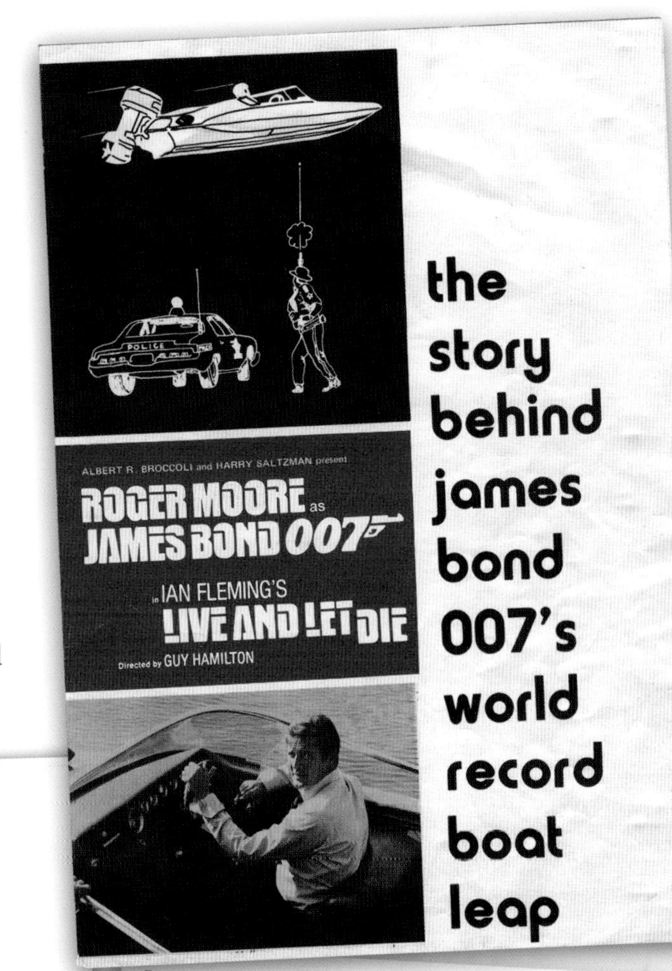

Left: The Glastron Boat Company published this brochure, promoting the role they played in the jump.

Below: "That there's one of them new car boats," says a Louisiana policemen, mocking the Sheriff's misfortune.

Left: Jerry Comeaux signed this photo of his record-breaking stunt. Gardner Schneider is on the stepladder and I'm bottom right, in the hat.

cake and demolishes the marquee. They were simply propelled at very high speed across the land.

One of our boats was being repaired, leaving three available to take part in the sequence. Jerry got in the first one, revved the engine, took off and promptly ploughed into a tree. He was injured, and now we were down to two boats. Another stunt driver took his place, and the guy chasing him slid straight across the lawn, colliding with another tree. He was knocked unconscious and the side of his boat was ripped out. As if that wasn't bad enough, in less than a minute someone ran up to him and stole the watch from his arm. Bill Treadway said, "We should have taken that tree out," but I told him we couldn't go uprooting trees on the off chance that one of them was going to get in the way. We decided to try again the following day, by which time one of the original boats would have been back from the workshop and we'd have also taken delivery of a new one from the manufacturer, Glastron.

Early the following morning I was woken by a phone call from Bill. "Pete – it's high tide and the whole of the peninsula is flooded. What should I do?" I asked him to save the wedding guests' folding chairs, because they were all rented, and told him to then call Derek Cracknell, the assistant director, to tell him what had happened. We managed to keep busy filming the police riverblock at Miller's Bridge, before returning to the Treadway Estate when the flood water had subsided.

This time, a stunt driver took the boat straight across the peninsula and back into the water on the other side. Despite my reassurances, I noticed Bill had dug up the tree previously hit by Jerry. It was just as well he'd ignored my advice, because the

Above left: A powerboat skids across the lawn, with terrible consequences for a wedding.

Top right: Jerry's boat, on a collision course with a tree.

Above right: Gardner, Peter and their daughter all took part in the filming.

LEFT AND FAR LEFT: Lakefront Airport played host to the Bleeker Flying School for one of the film's more lighthearted sequences.

BELOW LEFT: Harry Saltzman maintains a watchful eye on proceedings, while Roger relaxes between takes.

BELOW RIGHT: One of Mr Big's henchmen collides with a Douglas DC-3 at the airport. This was the plane we purchased for $500.

trajectory of the new boat was exactly the same and there would have been another collision. A driver called Eddie Smith then performed the wedding demolition, bringing his boat up onto the land before sending it through the cake and into the marquee.

The sequence where Bond commandeers a plane to escape from Mr Big's thugs was filmed at Lakefront Airport. We had to trash this plane, and a number of others, in the mayhem that ensued. Harry Saltzman, who had been with the main unit throughout the New Orleans shoot, told me it was easy to pick up old planes for no more than $500. Well, I eventually managed to find one for that price, but then I had to pay an extra $5,000 to have it restored so it passed muster on screen. I showed Harry a picture and told him, "This is what a $500 plane looks like." I then showed him the results of the renovation. "And this is what a $500 plane looks like when it's done up. Except now it's cost $6,000." Finally, I showed him a $4,500 plane that didn't need any work at all. He eventually got the point that it had ultimately cost more to buy a wreck than to buy a decent one.

Location filming moved to Jamaica at the end of 1972. A crocodile farm owned by American stuntman Ross Kananga was

one of our principal locations, posing as New Orleans. I knew we were in for an interesting time when I noticed the sign on the gate read 'Trespassers Will Be Eaten'.

In the film, Bond is abandoned by Tee Hee (Julius W Harris) on a small island circled by crocodiles. Ross anchored three of the crocodiles down and doubled for Roger as he jumped across their backs to reach the safety of the bank on the other side. You'll notice the third crocodile turns around to snap at his ankle. Perhaps unsurprisingly, we only filmed this scene once.

Harry's economy drive continued while we were in Jamaica. Everyone started getting lunch boxes that contained a sandwich, some lettuce, an orange and an apple. There were a lot of complaints and I was nominated to raise the issue with Harry. I didn't see why it was my responsibility – I was supposed to be the art director – but I had a word with him anyway. "We spent all the money in New Orleans," he protested, insisting that these meagre lunchboxes were the best he could do. George Crawford, the caterer, asked me how I got on and I told him Harry wouldn't budge. Shortly afterwards Harry went to George to get his lunch. He was handed a lunchbox containing a lettuce leaf, an apple and a tin of sardines with no key. The next day, proper lunches were reinstated for everyone.

I wondered if the pressure was getting to Harry – while we were out there he dismissed the set decorator Simon Wakefield for reasons I never discovered. This left me covering a lot of Simon's duties in addition to my own work. When we were in New Orleans Cubby joined the shoot much later than Harry. Shortly after they arrived, Cubby and his wife Dana decided to throw an impromptu party because they thought everyone looked so miserable.

We returned to Pinewood in the last week of December, filming interiors on Syd Cain's sets before and after the Christmas break. Early in 1973 Guy called me into his office and said, "Pack a bag – you're going to New York." I had been under the impression that Syd was going to handle the filming in Harlem, but Guy told me he wanted me to go instead.

Top: A publicity shot of Roger and Jane Seymour (as Solitaire), taken at Pinewood in early 1973.

Above: I was careful not to get too close when I photographed the crocodiles at Ross Kananga's Jungle Swamp Safari.

Right and far right: The wooden bridge retracts and Bond comes up with a daring way to escape the advancing crocodiles.

FAR LEFT: The Fillet of Soul restaurant in Harlem, where Bond meets Solitaire.

LEFT: The customised Cadillac we hired for use as a pimpmobile in the film.

BELOW: Reconnaissance photos of Broad and South Streets in Manhattan, where Bond crashes his car after his driver is assassinated.

New York was freezing, but I was rather better prepared for the low temperatures than I had been during my *Thunderball* stopover. I met up with Steve Hendrickson and Charlie Russhon in Manhattan. This was where the 'blaxploitation' theme of *Live and Let Die* really came to the fore, as Harry gave us instructions to find a 'pimpmobile' for Mr Big's henchman Whisper (Earl Jolly Brown). Harry was sending us to Harlem, and thought the neighbourhood was so dangerous that he promised us a bodyguard. We waited for a while but the guy didn't turn up, so we decided to take our chances on our own.

We were on the corner of 105th and Lenox when Steve spotted a customised Cadillac with a low roof, owned by a flamboyant pimp covered in gold chains. Steve went over to talk to him, and he agreed to hire the car to us for as long as we needed it. Shortly after we returned to our hotel we found out why our bodyguard never turned up – he had been on the subway, reading a book of poetry, when thieves took his money and his train ticket, undid his trousers and ran off.

The pimpmobile is first seen on FDR Drive, as Whisper cruises alongside Bond's car and uses a dart gun built into the wing mirror to kill Bond's driver. (The

TOP LEFT AND ABOVE: The location of the Oh Cult Voodoo Shop at East 65th Street, before and after dressing.

TOP RIGHT: Bond follows Kananga's trail to the shop.

RIGHT: Our vantage point for the 69th Street building we used as the San Monique Consulate in New York.

wing mirror was a special prop designed by Derek for the close-ups.) The car then veers across the road until Bond brings it back under control.

The early part of the sequence, before the assassination, was shot from a vantage point overlooking FDR Drive. We didn't tell the police what we were doing because at that stage we were only filming one car gradually drawing closer to another. I was joined by Dick Kratina, the cameraman I'd last seen in Bermuda during the making of *You Only Live Twice*. We shone a light from our window to give the drivers of the two cars a signal that Dick was ready.

For the latter part of the sequence, where Bond's car swerves across the road, the police agreed to close FDR Drive for four hours on a Sunday morning. When the day arrived we were forced to cancel our plans because a thick fog had descended. The police kindly said that if we came back on Tuesday they'd stop the traffic from 11 to 2 o'clock to allow our convoy through. This meant we'd be asking the crew to work through lunch, so Guy asked Mike Rauch, the New York location manager, to make sure everyone was fed. On Tuesday morning I accompanied Mike to a little deli. "How many sandwiches do you want?" asked the girl behind the counter. "108," said Mike. She stared at him for a moment before saying, "You'll have to come behind the counter to help me."

Bond's first meeting with Mr Big (Yaphet Kotto) memorably ends with the villain telling his henchmen to "take this honky out and waste him." We found some derelict buildings in Harlem, and Guy said it was the ideal location. We fixed up the fire escape, which Bond pulls down to knock out one of the thugs, and then Guy noticed a number of wires hanging between the buildings. He wanted to include them in shot, and in the film you can see Bond sweep some of them out of his way. We cut a bunch of these wires down and moved them into position. On the morning we were due to shoot the scene, a couple of fellas turned up, asking to speak to whoever was in charge. Their red-and-gold hats indicated that they were telephone engineers. "Someone round here's been messing around with the lines," said one of them angrily, before pointing to the wires leading into the derelict buildings. "Up until yesterday all these worked." We maintained an embarrassed silence as they climbed ladders to begin their work.

The *Live and Let Die* shoot had been tough at times, but Roger Moore was a good man to have as the head of your company when things got tricky. Kind, courteous and always good-humoured, he was popular with all of us. He may not have been as athletic as either of his predecessors, but he was the right man for the role and I was pleased when I found out he'd be returning for *The Man With the Golden Gun*.

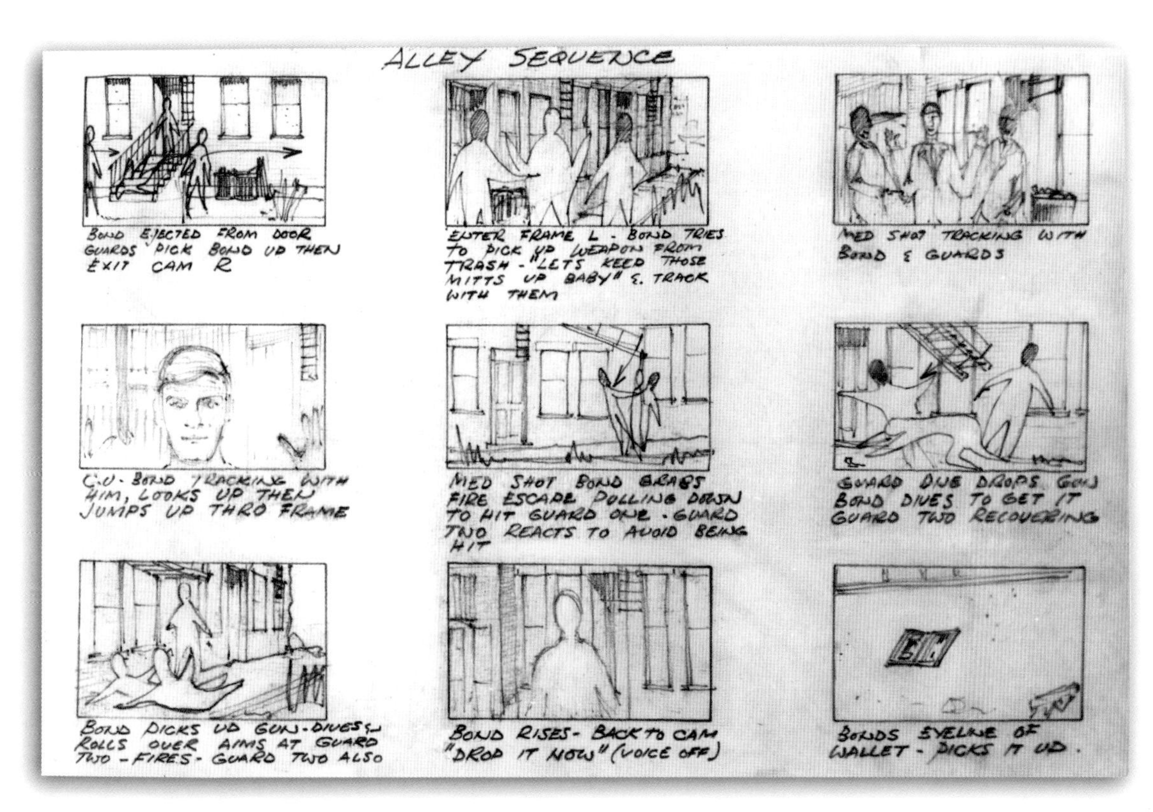

1. CRASH SITE (MEET POLICE DEPARTMENT: 9:30am)
2. HOUSTON STREET TO CRASH SITE
3. VOODOO SHOP AND GARAGE
4. CONSULATE
5. LEITER'S APARTMENT
6. FILLET OF SOUL AND ALLEY
7. CENTRAL PARK
8. HARLEM
9. TRIBORO BRIDGE
10. PAN AM TERMINAL - JFK AIRPORT

IAN FLEMING'S "LIVE AND LET DIE" – JAMES BOND 007

NEW ORLEANS
EON PRODUCTIONS LTD. "LIVE AND LET DIE"
618 DUMAINE STREET, NEW ORLEANS, LOUISIANA 70116
TELEPHONE: 504-529-3544 CABLE ADDRESS: LETLIVE NLN

EON PRODUCTIONS LTD
1 TILNEY STREET, LONDON W1Y 5LE, ENGLAND
CABLE ADDRESS: TILNEYFILM

UNITED ARTISTS CORPORATION
729 SEVENTH AVENUE, NEW YORK, N.Y.

LEFT: My storyboards of the sequence in Harlem where Bond uses the fire escape to escape from Mr Big's thugs.

ABOVE: Roger and Harry on location for *Live and Let Die*. Lon Satton, who played CIA agent Harold Strutter, is in the background.

RIGHT: My list of locations for the New York shoot in early 1973.

THE MAN WITH THE GOLDEN GUN

Cubby and Harry had originally wanted to film *The Man With the Golden Gun*, Ian Fleming's final novel, in the late 1960s. The idea was resurrected in the early 70s, and I remember Harry mentioning it to Roger Moore while we were making *Live and Let Die*.

1973 was the year of Bruce Lee's *Enter the Dragon*, and the martial arts craze had a big influence on *The Man With the Golden Gun*, a film that took us to the Far East after several years of principally North American locations. Guy Hamilton, returning for his fourth and final Bond, joined Cubby for a reconnaissance of Phuket and some of the other islands off the southern coast of Thailand in October.

Peter Murton came back to the art department, this time as production designer, and it was good to see him again. He asked John Graysmark and me to be the art directors. John's father had been the construction manager at MGM's studio in Borehamwood, while his own career as a draughtsman had included everything from *Summer Holiday* (1963) to *2001: A Space Odyssey* (1968). John's brother Tony is a construction manager who would later work on a quite a few Bond films. In fact he's still one of my best friends – we have dinner every Friday.

Khao Phing Kan, an island in the Phuket province, would become the hideaway of the film's villain, Francisco Scaramanga (Christopher Lee). Peter sent John and me on a two-week recce to Thailand and Hong Kong. As he handed us the details he said, "Be prepared to stay." He wasn't kidding – I came home seven months later. This was the age before emails or even faxes. A telex took three days and most of the time I wasn't even able to find a phone. I kept in touch with my long-suffering wife, Ann, and our children, Madelaine and Neil, by sending postcards as often as I could.

In all aspects of culture, communication and geography, Thailand felt like the other side of the world. There was a plane in and out of Phuket island once a day, and if you weren't booked into one of its three seats then you were left hoping you'd be able to get on the next one. Khao Phing Kan was stunning but unsurprisingly deserted. Gazing out from the shore we could see the waves lapping at the tapered

OPPOSITE PAGE: Christopher Lee with the golden gun I designed for his character Scaramanga.

ABOVE: Members of the design team on location in 1974. From left to right – me, Peter Childs, Michael Redding, John Graysmark, Les Dilley and Ernest Archer.

base of a tall, limestone outcrop that we later discovered was called Ko Tapu. This would also feature prominently in the film as, in the words of Scaramanga, the "mushroom-shaped rock" that housed the solar panels for his energy weapon.

Moving on to Hong Kong was another culture shock. We were picked up in green Rolls-Royces and chauffeured to the five-star Peninsula Hotel. Wherever you went in the room a boy would beat you there with hot tea. The place seemed deserted until you reached any door, which would magically open to reveal someone eager to take care of you.

As well as shooting on the streets of Hong Kong, we conducted some preliminary photography at the ocean liner *Queen Elizabeth*, which had capsized in the harbour in 1972. In the film, the wreck would become the unlikely location of M's Hong Kong office.

The estate owned by Hai Fat (Richard Loo) was a location belonging to a local entrepreneur called Mr Lee. The mausoleum where Hai Fat was eventually buried was real. The scenes with the sumo wrestlers on the estate were largely inspired by the look of the Tiger Balm Gardens in Singapore, which Peter

TOP: Replica temples in Mueang Boran, a place just outside Bangkok known to tourists as the Ancient City. This was where we filmed the sequence at the school of martial arts.

RIGHT: Ko Tapu, the outcrop we noticed from the shore of Khao Phing Kan.

FAR RIGHT: The islands as they appear in the film. The outcrop housed Scaramanga's solar collector.

Murton had asked me to visit as part of our research.

Peter was the head of a large group, all working on props and drawings. As well as myself there was assistant art director Ernie Archer, draughtsman John Fenner, set dresser Peter Howitt, construction manager Michael Redding and many others. Ernie had been my tutor when I learned to draw at Pinewood in the 1950s, and although this was his first film as assistant art director we knew each other very well. He was the most fabulous draughtsman you could ever hope to meet – every drawing was amazing.

While we were in Hong Kong we made a trip out to Macau, where we conducted our recce riding in rickshaws. Peter then sent me back to Phuket to work on Scaramanga's Chinese junk. Although I was the art director I found myself fulfilling quite a few other roles for the crew while I was there – everything from transportation to catering seemed to become my responsibility. If a hotel manager said he was fully booked I'd say, "No you're not – you can put him in with him and her in with her – now you've got two spare rooms!" At one point I even had to go to the Chinese pharmacy on behalf of someone who had the runs.

Rather than building a junk from scratch we brought an old boat up from Kuala

TOP LEFT: The ocean liner *Queen Elizabeth* caught fire in Hong Kong harbour in 1972 and capsized as a result. She was scrapped shortly after we shot the film.

ABOVE: Standing on Scaramanga's junk at the beginning of the boat's restoration.

LEFT: A picture taken while restoration was underway.

FAR LEFT: The finished boat, in a scene from the film.

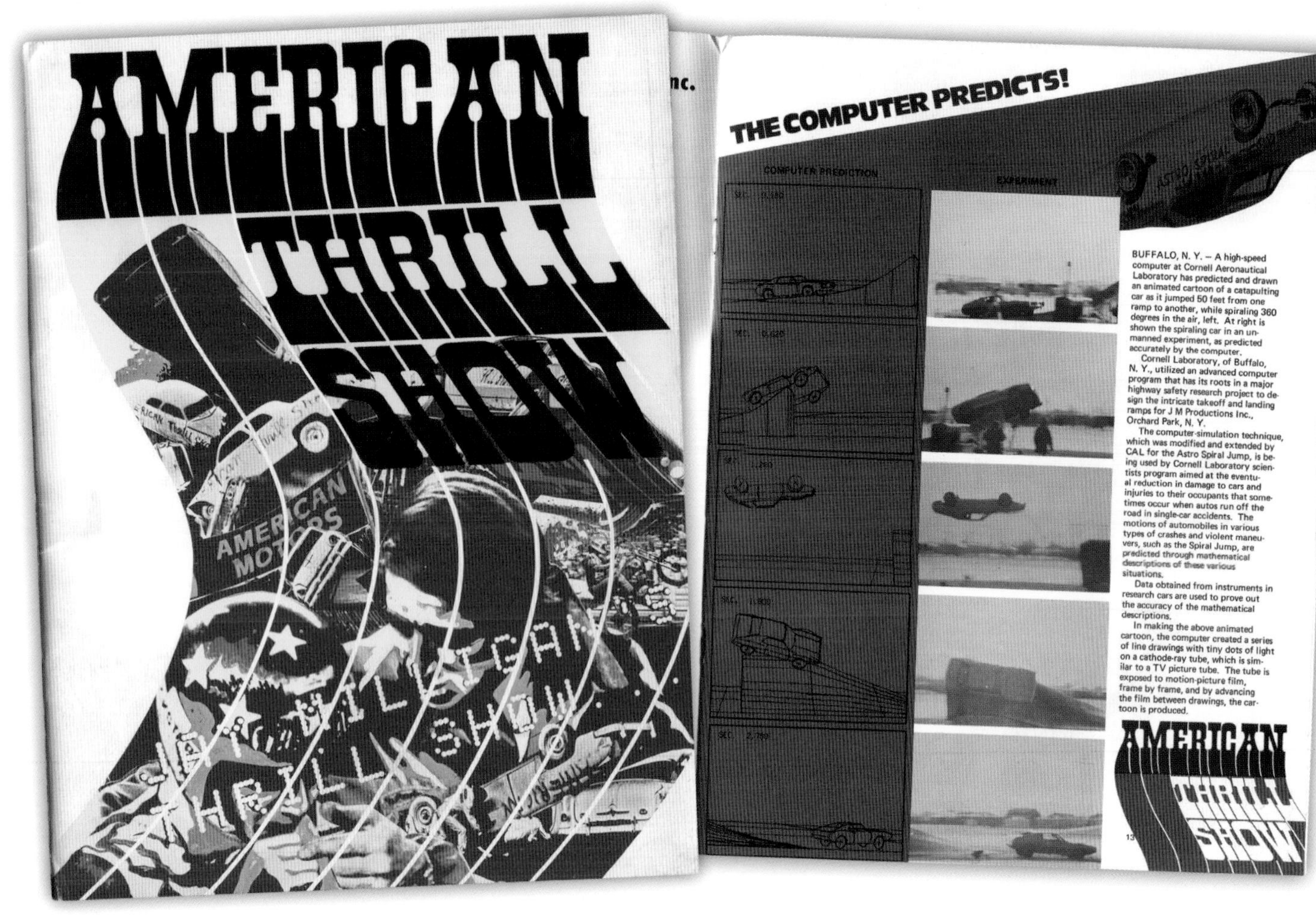

AMERICAN THRILL SHOW

THE COMPUTER PREDICTS!

COMPUTER PREDICTION

EXPERIMENT

BUFFALO, N. Y. – A high-speed computer at Cornell Aeronautical Laboratory has predicted and drawn an animated cartoon of a catapulting car as it jumped 50 feet from one ramp to another, while spiraling 360 degrees in the air, left. At right is shown the spiraling car in an unmanned experiment, as predicted accurately by the computer.

Cornell Laboratory, of Buffalo, N. Y., utilized an advanced computer program that has its roots in a major highway safety research project to design the intricate takeoff and landing ramps for J M Productions Inc., Orchard Park, N. Y.

The computer-simulation technique, which was modified and extended by CAL for the Astro Spiral Jump, is being used by Cornell Laboratory scientists program aimed at the eventual reduction in damage to cars and injuries to their occupants that sometimes occur when autos run off the road in single-car accidents. The motions of automobiles in various types of crashes and violent maneuvers, such as the Spiral Jump, are predicted through mathematical descriptions of these various situations.

Data obtained from instruments in research cars are used to prove out the accuracy of the mathematical descriptions.

In making the above animated cartoon, the computer created a series of line drawings with tiny dots of light on a cathode-ray tube, which is similar to a TV picture tube. The tube is exposed to motion-picture film, frame by frame, and by advancing the film between drawings, the cartoon is produced.

AMERICAN THRILL SHOW

Lumpur to renovate it. This seemed like a good idea until I saw the state of the thing and realised how filthy it was. It was a labour-intensive job, but the Phuket craftsmen we employed were amazing. They used curved blades to make precise adjustments to the wood, taking a sliver off at a time if necessary. They nailed scaffolding to the hull of the boat so they could crawl all over it, but at one point there were so many people that the scaffolding collapsed into the sea.

I had new sails made and they were decorated by an English painter called Pat Joy, one of the crew members staying with John's team in Phang Nga. This would have been fine, were it not for the fact that I'd only wanted the sails to be stained with dirty water. When I found out what Pat had done I threw them into the sea to try to clean them, jumping overboard in a frantic effort to get the paint off.

Cubby had loved the powerboat jump in *Live and Let Die*, and the somersaulting car in *The Man With the Golden Gun* was an attempt to go one better. Following an improbable reunion with a holidaying JW Pepper (Clifton James), drastic measures are required to catch up with Scaramanga and his diminutive manservant Nick Nack (Hervé Villechaize) on the other side of a khlong. Bond spots the twisted remnants of a broken bridge and tells Pepper, "Ever heard of Evel Knievel?" The car accelerates, somersaulting over the gap in the bridge before landing on all four wheels on the other side.

The sequence originated in the 'Astro Spiral Jump' – a stunt performed by Jay Milligan as part of an event called The American Thrill Show. Cubby had seen footage of the jump performed at the Houston Astrodome and asked Milligan if the same stunt could be performed over water. While extremely dangerous,

ABOVE: Pages from the brochure promoting the American Thrill Show. A computer at the Cornell Aeronautical Laboratory calculated the trajectory of Jay Milligan's incredible car stunt.

RIGHT: 'Bumps' Willert next to the specially converted AMC Hornet he drove over the bridge.

FAR RIGHT: Although the bridge looked rickety, the ramp was wade of concrete.

the twisting ramps on either side, the spiralling trajectory of the car and its landing spot were all mathematically calculated with the help of a computer at the Cornell Aeronautical Laboratory in Buffalo. As part of an investigation into road safety, they'd discovered that if a car on the freeway hit a ramp at a certain speed then it could do a 360-degree flip and end up back on its wheels.

The stunt could be repeated any number of times but it required careful preparation. American Motors provided us with three cars – two in Bangkok and one in the US in case we needed it. They had to widen each car by a few inches and centralise all the controls. Then we asked them to add a fifth wheel to the back axel, giving the car the extra bit of propulsion it needed to lift away from the first ramp and make the twist. The bridge looked rickety on screen, and the car looked quite ordinary, but the ramps were made of concrete and everything had to be precision-built or adapted.

We shot the stunt outside Bangkok in early June 1974. The driver was Loren 'Bumps' Willert, a guy brought over by Jay Milligan. He only did it once and we got exactly what we needed. The whole thing ended up costing $300,000 but Cubby thought it was money well spent. There were some police cars chasing Bond, and afterwards Cubby told me it would have been great to have them go over the bridge as well. Unfortunately there was just no time, and sending one car over had already taken a lot of our resources.

Later in June we moved back to Pinewood for the interior filming, which included one of my favourite parts of the film. Scaramanga's golden gun was represented by three props – two were solid and one could be broken down to its various components. The barrel was a

Above left: Bumps and John Graysmark by the receiving ramp.

Above centre: A view of the exit ramp on the other side of the water.

Above right: Michael Redding and John Graysmark, who were responsible for constructing the ramps.

Below left: Bond's car achieves the seemingly impossible in these pictures from the film. The stunt was captured on the first and only take.

Right and far right: Scaramanga assembles the golden gun as he prepares to assassinate Hai Fat. I showed Christopher Lee how the pieces clipped together and he practised until he could do it without looking.

Below: Harry Saltzman and Cubby Broccoli had produced the Bond films since 1962, but this would be their last picture together.

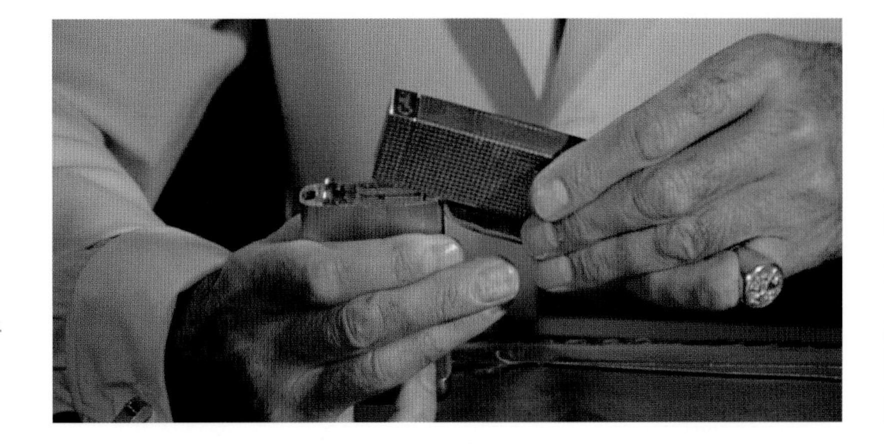

Waterman Gentleman fountain pen, the bullet chamber was a Colibri cigarette lighter, the handle was a cigarette case and the trigger was a cuff link.

Before I left England I'd taken my original design to Colibri, showing them a drawing of a wooden mock-up of the gun. When I reached Hong Kong I received a message from Cubby, who said Colibri had got back to them with a quote that was far too expensive. I told Cubby that when I visited Colibri I'd asked them if they needed an official order to make the prop and they'd said no. I'd also asked them if they wanted any money and they'd similarly declined. Ernie Archer was still in England at that time, so he and Ronnie Quelch visited Colibri to take all the materials back. Ronnie knew a wholesale jeweller with a workshop off Tottenham Court Road. He asked them to fit all the components together and they made the solid props as well, each one crafted from gold-plated silver.

We see Scaramanga assemble the gun right in front of one of his victims. As Hai Fat is admonishing him, Scaramanga flips up the end of his cigarette case, slides the extended lighter onto the top of the case and screws in the fountain pen. With the gun complete, he aims the weapon at Hai Fat and calmly pulls the trigger. According to the story, Scaramanga had been a professional assassin since the late 1950s, so it was important that Christopher Lee was able to assemble the gun in a casual manner, without spending too long looking down at what he was doing. He was able to achieve this by copying the way I did it. Before the scene was filmed at Pinewood he came to my office in the art department and said, "I've got all the pieces in front of me on the desk but I

Harry had got himself into a lot of financial difficulty by having fingers in too many pies, the latest of which was his troubled ownership of Technicolor. He also had a lot of personal problems. His wife, Jacqueline, was diagnosed with cancer in the early 1970s; when we were doing *Live and Let Die* in New York Harry asked

don't know how to put them together." So we chatted for a while about which component went where, and then I showed him how it was done. I used to take the gun home in the evenings, practising taking it apart and putting it back together while I was watching television. Christopher asked if he could take it home and do the same thing. By the time he brought it back he had it down to a tee. Some actors are lousy with props, but he did it beautifully.

Despite this and other highlights, *The Man With the Golden Gun* didn't perform as well as any of its predecessors when it opened in December 1974. I don't know if this had any bearing on what happened next. In November the following year Harry Saltzman declared his intention to sell his 50 per cent share of the James Bond film rights to Columbia. This came as news to Cubby, who only found out when a journalist from *Variety* told him.

me to bring some drugs back to England for her.

Harry eventually sold his stake in Bond to Cubby's distributor, United Artists, in December 1975. I only saw him once after that, when we bumped into each other at a craft fair in Denham Village Hall. He'd recently suffered a stroke, but was well enough to spend some time reminiscing fondly about the old days.

In 1975 I had mixed feelings about losing one of our producers. Harry was a nice man, but I didn't miss him. There was so much angst between him and Cubby that I think it was better for Cubby to go it alone.

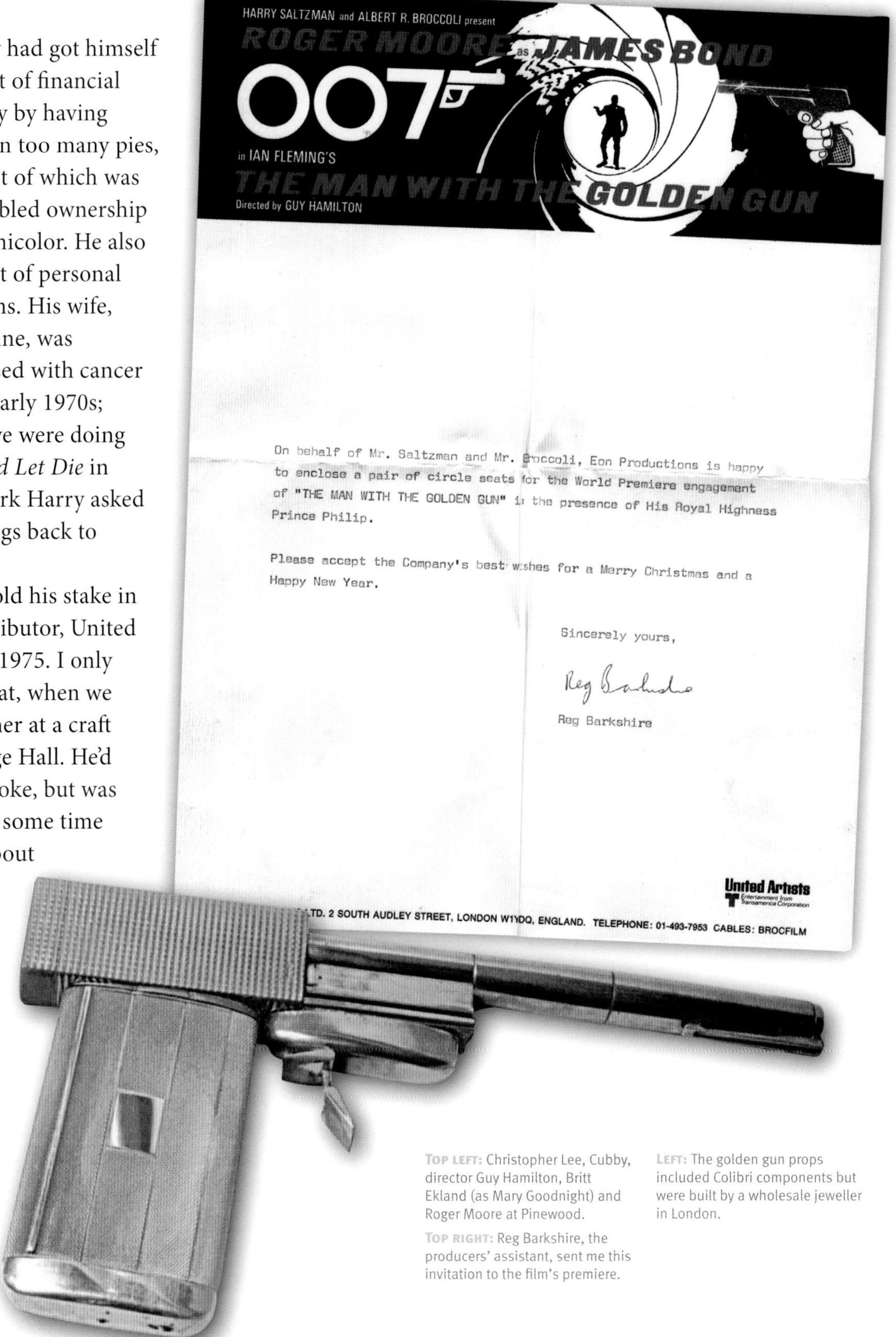

HARRY SALTZMAN and ALBERT R. BROCCOLI present
ROGER MOORE as JAMES BOND
007
in IAN FLEMING'S
THE MAN WITH THE GOLDEN GUN
Directed by GUY HAMILTON

On behalf of Mr. Saltzman and Mr. Broccoli, Eon Productions is happy to enclose a pair of circle seats for the World Premiere engagement of "THE MAN WITH THE GOLDEN GUN" in the presence of His Royal Highness Prince Philip.

Please accept the Company's best wishes for a Merry Christmas and a Happy New Year.

Sincerely yours,

Reg Barkshire

United Artists
Entertainment from Transamerica Corporation

...LTD. 2 SOUTH AUDLEY STREET, LONDON W1YDQ, ENGLAND. TELEPHONE: 01-493-7953 CABLES: BROCFILM

Top left: Christopher Lee, Cubby, director Guy Hamilton, Britt Ekland (as Mary Goodnight) and Roger Moore at Pinewood.

Top right: Reg Barkshire, the producers' assistant, sent me this invitation to the film's premiere.

Left: The golden gun props included Colibri components but were built by a wholesale jeweller in London.

THE SPY WHO LOVED ME

The dispute between Harry and Cubby, and the emerging threat of a rival Bond movie by *Thunderball* producer Kevin McClory, resulted in a longer-than-usual delay between *The Man With the Golden Gun* and the next James Bond film. I kept busy in the intervening years, working as the art director on a film called *Inside Out* (1975), directed by Peter Duffell, and the Sherlock Holmes film *The Seven-Per-Cent Solution* (1976), directed by Herbert Ross.

By 1976 Cubby was ready to relaunch the Bond films in spectacular style with *The Spy Who Loved Me*. At nearly $14 million, the budget of the new picture was almost double what *The Man With the Golden Gun* had cost. The film would bring us back to the epic, ambitious style of *You Only Live Twice*. The production designer of that film, Ken Adam, and its director, Lewis Gilbert, would be returning.

Our initial reconnaissance was conducted at Okinawa in Japan, and on the way we picked up the screenwriter Christopher Wood, who lived in Copenhagan. At the Expo in Okinawa we saw a huge aquarium made of Plexiglass, and this prompted ideas for the decor of Atlantis, the undersea base occupied by the film's villain, Stromberg (Curt Jürgens).

The Spy Who Loved Me's Egyptian locations included the pyramids, the Sphinx, the Giza Necropolis and a trip down the Nile – altogether some of the most breathtaking scenery in any Bond film. Together with Cubby, Lewis and associate producer Bill Cartlidge, I flew into Cairo on a VC10. When we arrived we were told we were the first film crew in Egypt since the death of President Nasser in 1970. I made the best of our trip, despite missing some of the entertainment when I succumbed to food poisoning. Particularly memorable were the Shifting Sands outside Cairo, where the wind stole my footprints moments after I made them.

Egypt was stunning, but the script called for a sequence set in and around the Giza Plateau at night. We weren't sure whether that would be possible because in 1976 film wasn't fast enough to capture such limited light in those conditions. Claude Renoir, our director of photography, came out, took one look at the Sphinx and the pyramids illuminated in the distance, and told us it was impossible.

I wondered whether my cousin, Alan Maley, might have the solution. Alan was a matte artist who began his career at Denham Studios in the 1950s. He'd since gone to Hollywood, winning an Oscar in 1972 for his special effects work on Disney's *Bedknobs and Broomsticks*. A lot of his techniques remained a mystery to me, because although he was my cousin and we got on, he could be

OPPOSITE PAGE: The interior of the *Liparus* supertanker was constructed at the same time as the 007 Stage.

ABOVE: Members of the special effects and art departments, including Derek Meddings, me, Richard Kennan, producer Cubby Broccoli, Michael Redding, Brian Savegar and Brian Smithies.

Right and opposite page: Shots of the 007 Stage under construction in summer 1976.

Below: Cubby and Pinewood's managing director Cyril Howard, who authorised the building of the stage.

a little bit secretive when it came to the tricks of his trade. Alan helped us enormously by finding a typically ingenious solution to the problem. As seen in the film, the pyramids look like a genuine night shot, but they were in fact models. In the first instance the scene was filmed with the audience watching the light show in the distance. The pyramids occupied the top half of the frame, which because of the low light levels was essentially unexposed. Alan matted off the bottom part of the picture, which comprised the audience and the Sphinx, and then filmed his models of the pyramids which had been lit by Robin Browne. He then seamlessly combined both shots – the audience and the Sphinx at the bottom and the models at the top – to create the entirely convincing illusion that we'd been able to shoot in impossibly low light.

Alan's sleight-of-hand was also applied to Stromberg's base, Atlantis. The base was mostly realised using Derek's models in the Bahamas and Alan's matte paintings – the only part of it that was built 'life size' was a small section that we placed in a lake outside Sardinia, for the scene where Bond's jet-ski approaches the base.

The location reconnaissance moved from Giza to Luxor, where I was ill again, before we returned to Cairo and headed back to England to deal with the studio photography.

The Spy Who Loved Me brought the plot of *You Only Live Twice* down to earth, or rather under the sea. In the previous film spaceships had been subsumed by SPECTRE's volcano base. This time round, a hollow supertanker would swallow up three nuclear submarines belonging to rival powers with the aim of provoking a world war.

Depicting the huge submarine dock inside the *Liparus* supertanker was clearly going to be a major challenge. Cubby knew someone who owned a real supertanker, so Bill Cartlidge went to South Africa to take a look at it. Even though it was due to be emptied, there was no way it was going to be practical for us to shoot all the action inside a real ship.

Our next thought was to build the submarine dock inside one of the former airship hangars at RAF Cardington in Bedfordshire, where some scenes in *Chitty Chitty Bang Bang* had been filmed. There are two of these 'sheds' at Cardington, and the one we looked at was 812 feet long, 180 feet wide and 157 feet high. At this time it still housed barrage balloons filled with hydrogen, so the RAF told us that our crew members would have to use copper-faced tools to ensure they didn't create any sparks. The sheer size of the shed, and the safety restrictions, clearly made it unsuitable for our purposes.

Above: The continuing construction of the set within the stage.

Below left: The cover design of this promotional brochure featured Ken Adam's sketch of the *Liparus* interior.

Below right: A blueprint of the stage.

Ken had considered the old Handley Page aircraft works in Radlett during pre-production of his previous film, *Barry Lyndon* (1975), but when we had a look at it we realised that wasn't suitable for us either because it was only around 30 feet high.

Ken came to the conclusion that the only solution was a purpose-built, silent stage, constructed over the tank at Pinewood. The length and width of the tank would partly dictate its dimensions. Ken designed the stage, and the interior set of the submarine dock, at the same time. Roy Dorman and Charles Bishop created the drawings for the *Liparus*, while Ken consulted Michael Brown and his father, the architects who had made the structural designs for the *You Only Live Twice* volcano, about the stage. They came back with a quote of £85,000, and I signed the order that began construction. Contrary to what was claimed at the time, we never sought permission to build anything permanent – in fact, the new stage would be classed as a temporary structure because it was designed to be rag-bolted to the ground. The bolts could be unscrewed and the whole building could be taken down.

The walls of the stage sloped in from the bottom to the top, creating something of a void between the edge of the tank and

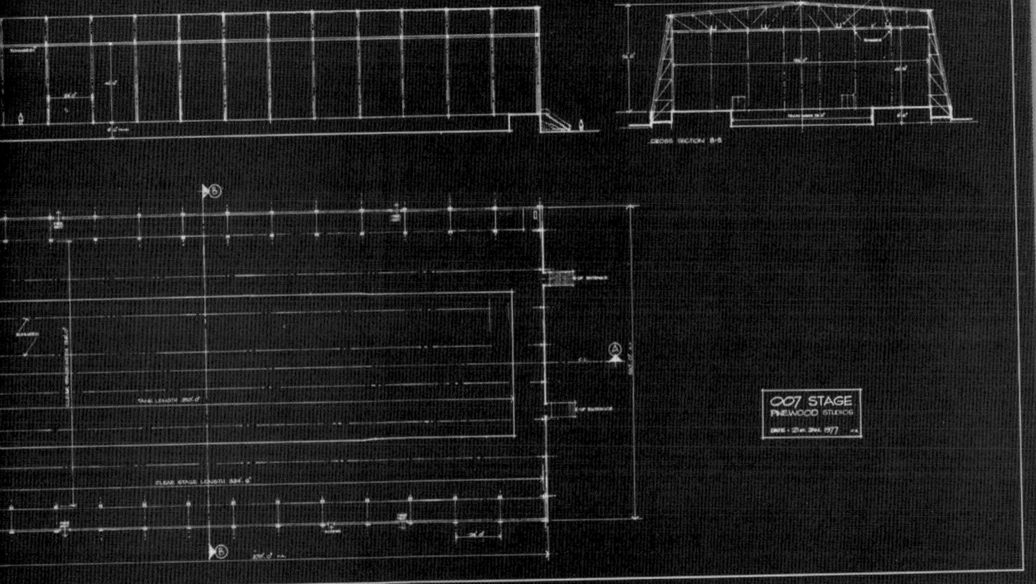

the base of the side walls. I tried to get Ed Chiltern, Pinewood's managing director, to fill in at least some of this space for us. Ed ran Pinewood on behalf of its owners, the Rank Organisation, and his attitude to my query said much about the state of the British film industry at the time. He dismissed my request, telling me he'd rather spend the money on bingo halls.

The stage took 13 weeks to construct, and the structural set inside was built concurrently. Ken was the captain of this project and he was in charge, but the first lieutenant runs a ship and you don't mess with him. I considered that I was Ken's first lieutenant during the construction of the new stage, but our relationship was sometimes fractious.

I would arrive early every morning and give instructions to the crew. Sometimes I'd return later in the day to discover that some of those orders had been countermanded. One of the things Ken complained about was the concrete floor not being polished earlier in the schedule. I said that you shouldn't put in a wet concrete floor and try to polish it while construction work was still going on elsewhere. I argued that we had to get the basic construction finished first – if we stopped to think about what the floor was going to look like we'd never get the roof on. We got there in the end, but I'm sorry to say that my relationship with Ken was starting to suffer.

The *Liparus* was supposed to capture three submarines – one British, one Soviet and one American – and in my capacity as art director I wanted to make sure that our representations of those submarines was as accurate as possible. We went on a research trip to the Royal Navy base at Faslane in Gare Loch, where we were

BELOW RIGHT: Ken and Cubby pictured during construction of the stage.

BOTTOM: The inside of the *Liparus* and the stolen submarines, as seen in the finished film.

BELOW LEFT: Barbara Bach (who played Anya Amasova), Roger Moore and former prime minister Harold Wilson officially opened the stage on 5 December 1976.

Above and below right: Five shots of Derek Meddings' models, showing the *Liparus* and the Atlantis base, all filmed in the Bahamas.

Below: Catch of the day!

invited on board the nuclear submarine *HMS Churchill*. At the weekend, a group of us went to Loch Long, where they loaded the nuclear weapons onto the submarines. We were allowed to photograph everything except one particular electronic board and incorporated as much as we could into the subsequent drawings. Much of what we saw was reproduced in the American submarine, in particular. One of the highlights of the trip for me was the chance to look around the Polaris submarine *HMS Renown*. The sub was gigantic, with three decks which I enjoyed exploring.

Despite all this research, I made a terrible blunder with the submarines captured by the *Liparus*, although I didn't realise it until much later. I insisted on a pennant number for the American sub. Being a smart-arse, I looked up its hunter-killer class in a copy of the reference book *Jane's Fighting Ships* and discovered that the number 593 was vacant. Richard Keenan, our naval adviser, told me he didn't think we should even use a pennant number but I overruled him because I felt the number would help the audience to distinguish one submarine from another.

Years later, Cubby told me about a letter he received from a viewer who felt our use of '593' had been in poor taste. He explained that the number had previously belonged to the *USS Thresher*, which in 1963 became the first nuclear submarine to be lost at sea. All 129 crew members died. It was only then that I realised why the number had been listed as vacant in *Jane's Fighting Ships* and I felt awful.

The framework and the moving systems inside the *Liparus* were made by Mike Hope, an engineer from Maidenhead. The speedboat that leaves the *Liparus* was propelled by a linear induction motor that enabled it to 'float' when the current was activated.

I've read that we chose the Lotus Esprit as Bond's car when we noticed one at the studio, but the car would never have been at the studio if I hadn't chosen it for the film in the first place. The Lotus Esprit S1 was launched in June 1976, a couple of months before principal photography started, but I'd already shown Ken a photo of the car in a magazine. The script called for a vehicle that Bond could take underwater, and I told Ken that I thought this could be just what we were looking for. Ken had previously owned a Lotus Elite and he liked the shape of the new Esprit. He did some sketches proposing how it could transform into a submarine. I took it upon myself to begin the negotiations with Lotus and was invited up to Hethel, the village in Norfolk where the company is based.

A lot of producers at that time would promise the sort of publicity money can't buy to get a car for a film, and then keep the car when filming was over. When I sat down with one of the Lotus executives I wondered if he suspected that this was my ploy. They told me straight away that they weren't going to give us a car. "All right then," I said. "Could you loan us one?" Silence. "Or hire one to us...?"

When I got back to Pinewood Ken asked me how I'd got on. I said I hoped I'd hear from them again, but I couldn't be sure. Two or three days later I got a call from Don McLaughlin, one of the executives, inviting me back to Hethel. He had some good news for me: "The chairman says I'm to help you in any way we can." I knew we'd need three cars – one for dry land, one to come out of the water and one to be modified by Derek Meddings to go underwater – so I started the ball rolling by asking for three bodies as soon as possible. Don said that three had recently come off the production line that weren't quite

LEFT: Barbara and Roger pose with the Lotus Esprit in the gardens at Pinewood.

BELOW: Q (Desmond Llewelyn) delivers the car to Bond in Sardinia.

RIGHT: In the Bahamas with the brilliant Derek Meddings.

FAR RIGHT: One of the Lotus shells, complete with Derek's modifications and Alka-Seltzer bubbles.

BELOW: Underwater filming in the Bahamas.

up to standard, so we could have those straight away. Don delivered the working car to Pinewood himself, and although it spent most of the time completely covered up, lots of people came out of their offices to look at it.

In the film, the car's journey off the beach and into the water began in Sardinia, where I had location-scouted with Cubby, Ken, and Ken's wife Letizia. When we arrived in Italy we stayed at the Grand Hotel in Rome. We had a wonderful evening there – I'd never tasted pasta like it – before flying to Sardinia and staying in the Hotel Cala di Volpe, the same place Bond (Roger Moore) and Anya (Barbara Bach) stay in the film.

We had to ask Lotus for a fourth car for the second-unit filming in Sardinia. I went back to Hethel where I was told it would be impossible to find yet another at such short notice. Then I remembered that the chairman, Colin Chapman, had one. And it was white – exactly the same colour as the others we had. In the end Lotus sent the car and two drivers to Sardinia, and it was these guys who were behind the wheel for the long shots. Colin even offered to send his private plane with spares for the car, but they performed so well that this wasn't necessary.

The scenes where the car was underwater were filmed in the Bahamas by Lamar Boren. Derek built three models at different sizes, but these were all 'wet' submarines with no air inside them. After a few minutes underwater the models wouldn't emit any of the air bubbles that would make them look like a convincing, pressurised submarine. Derek's solution was simple – he planted Alka-Seltzer tablets at hidden points around the models. These fizzed when they were submerged, creating an on-screen effect that was indistinguishable from the air bubbles you'd expect to see escaping from a real submarine.

Perry Oceanographics, a company of marine engineers, fitted engines to the third car after they had towed it through the water to ensure that it performed like a submarine. The retractable wheels and rotating fins were activated by nothing more sophisticated than Derek twiddling a broomstick out of shot.

LEFT AND FAR LEFT: Shots of the full-size submarine set being built at Selsey, on the Sussex coast.

BELOW LEFT, CENTRE AND RIGHT: The submarine was built on barrels and floated offshore.

Unfortunately bad weather in the Bahamas slowed up the shooting and United Artists started getting anxious. Dan Risner, the UA rep, asked me to go and sort it out. "You know everybody out there," he said. "Take it over and run it until they're back on schedule."

Golda Offenheim was our production secretary in the Bahamas and I didn't dare tell her what I'd been sent to do. Derek and the special effects boys were also there, wondering why the hell someone from the art department had suddenly turned up. Shortly after I arrived another day was abandoned and I wondered if we could get more done by moving to the other side of the island, where the weather was a bit better. So I made the suggestion, at no time revealing that I was on a mission for our distributor.

As soon as we moved to the new location we started picking up days. The mood lifted, we had some good times and got the job done. On the way back everyone packed their left-over booze into a container that we were sending back to Bristol. I told Golda that anything like that should go at the front of the container, not at the back, because we'd have to make it easily accessible to any customs officer that wanted to have a look. Bill Cartlidge looked a bit embarrassed when he heard about this, and sure enough we were accused of smuggling a commercial quantity of alcohol into the country. My name wasn't attached to any of the booze in the container, but we all had to share

BELOW LEFT: Me, Cubby, director Lewis Gilbert, Ken and our Egyptian production manager Ahmed Sami being entertained on the first reconnaissance to Giza.

BELOW RIGHT: Richard Kiel as Jaws. Richard's metal teeth were specially made by the dental technician Peter Thomas.

responsibility when we inevitably got busted. We were let off lightly with an £85 fine, which I paid.

Viewing *The Spy Who Loved Me* today, the inside of the *Liparus* and the Atlantis base are still impressive, but in some ways the biggest presence is that of a person, not a set. Jaws, the 7' 2" thug employed to pursue and kill Bond, was played by a gentle giant called Richard Kiel. Richard was a lovely man, who would often join us in the Red Lion just outside Slough for lunch. The first time we went I noticed he had to stoop to get through the door frame. Then he ordered two meals at the same time – presumably the habits of a lifetime.

Aside from his height, Jaws' distinctive feature – and the only part of the screenplay taken from Ian Fleming's novel – was a pair of steel-capped teeth that he could use to bite through solid objects or to murder his opponents. I asked my friend Peter Thomas, who was a dental technician, to make the teeth for me as a pair of chrome-cobalt dentures that clipped on to Richard's own teeth. When they were ready Peter came to the studio and showed Richard how to fit them. As soon as Richard smiled, revealing these rows of shining metal teeth, he looked very sinister.

Although they were incredible, the teeth were very uncomfortable and must have tasted awful. Richard could only keep them in for short periods but I never once heard him complain. Richard's scenes are some of the best in the film, including the chase in Giza, the fight in the train and his confrontation with Bond in Atlantis towards the end. Bond activates an electro-magnet that hoists Jaws up by his teeth. Bond leaves him dangling over the water, before switching off the current. Jaws drops into the water, leaving him at the mercy of a circling shark.

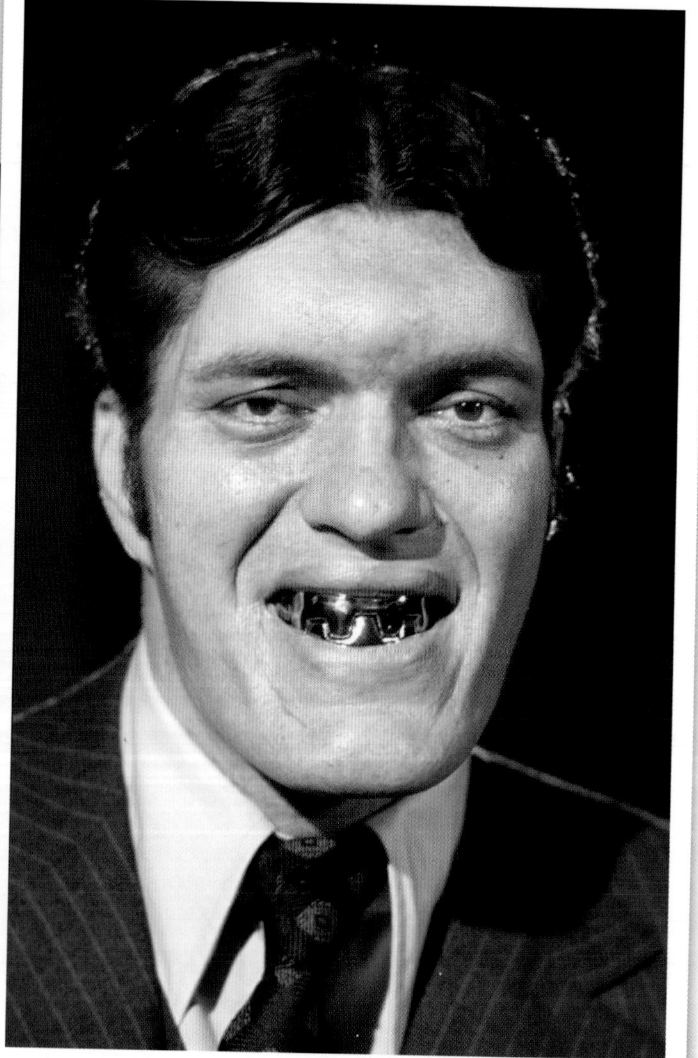

I was walking past the set when that sequence was being filmed and I bumped into Ken coming the other way. He had a frown on his face so I asked him what was wrong. "We can't find a line," he said, explaining that the humorous quip Bond usually uttered in these situations was eluding everybody. I followed Ken onto the set, where Cubby was sitting, looking equally vexed. Cubby always used to say that if anyone had an idea or something to contribute, however daft it might seem, then they should speak up. So I said, "I've got the line." Everyone looked at me in anticipation. "Bond activates the magnet, which picks up Jaws and leaves him hanging in mid-air. Bond gazes up at him and says, 'How does that grab you?'" The line made it into the picture, delivered by Roger with characteristic aplomb.

The production of *The Spy Who Loved Me* was long and demanding, but the result was a big hit with critics and audiences, putting the Bond films back on track. My relationship with Ken had been strained by the building of the new stage, which was formally opened as the 007 Stage on 5 December 1976, when shooting was over. There had been further angst over the Bahamas shoot, when he told me that I should have kept him better informed about progress on the delayed underwater filming. I argued that this had simply been a breakdown in communication between our respective offices, but he was still angry.

Along with the set decorator Hugh Scaife, Ken and I were nominated for an Academy Award for *The Spy Who Loved Me*. I had previously been nominated for *Fiddler on the Roof* in 1972 and I hoped this would be second time lucky. Ken and I remained on good terms after *The Spy Who Loved Me*, but the next Bond film would be our last together.

ABOVE LEFT: Being presented to the Princess Royal at the Leicester Square Odeon. Derek is next to me and Caroline Munro (who played Naomi) is in the background.

ABOVE RIGHT: My ticket to the premiere.

LEFT AND FAR LEFT: "How does that grab you?" Bond hoists Jaws to the ceiling using an electro-magnet.

MOONRAKER

MOONRAKER

The closing credits of *The Spy Who Loved Me* declared that James Bond would return in *For Your Eyes Only*, an adaptation of one of Ian Fleming's short stories. In 1978 a combination of science fiction and science fact prompted a change of direction.

The incredible success of George Lucas' *Star Wars* (1977) and Steven Spielberg's *Close Encounters of the Third Kind* (1977) helped to initiate a new kind of blockbuster, while away from the fantasy of cinema many people eagerly awaited the imminent launch of the Space Shuttle, NASA's most significant development since the first Moon landing almost a decade earlier. The next James Bond film would combine the best of all these worlds in a free adaptation of Fleming's novel *Moonraker*. The film would be scripted by Christopher Wood and directed by Lewis Gilbert, the same partnership that had revitalised the Bond series with *The Spy Who Loved Me*.

Sending Bond into space was never going to be cheap. *Moonraker* would have a bigger budget than *The Spy Who Loved Me*, but when pre-production began in 1978 I don't think any of us could have predicted just how much it would actually end up costing.

As well as spiralling costs, punitive levels of taxation were making things difficult for Eon's highest earners. It was around this time that Cubby reluctantly left London, moving to Beverly Hills in California. Soon afterwards the decision was taken to produce *Moonraker* outside the UK – interiors would be filmed across three studios in France, with Pinewood retained only for the special effects unit.

Ken Adam decided to take only one art director from the UK, and much to my regret he decided that it wouldn't be me. He instead chose my colleague Charles Bishop, but thanks to an intervention from Lewis I retained a role as 'visual effects art director', staying in the UK for much of the shooting, working alongside Derek Meddings.

I was dismayed by Ken's decision because, aside from our long relationship, I had participated in so many of the location reconnaissance trips in 1978. These began in the United States in the spring, and as a precursor Cubby said we should attend the 50th Academy Awards ceremony because we'd been nominated for *The Spy Who Loved Me*. "Let's mix business with pleasure," he suggested, so in March I flew out with Derek and special effects cameraman Robin Browne. When we arrived at the Beverly Boulevard

OPPOSITE PAGE: Filming Drax's space station at Pinewood. The space station was designed by Ken Adam and embellished by Harry Lange, one of the art directors. The model was built by visual effects supervisor Derek Meddings.

ABOVE: Roger Moore as James Bond, in one of the space station interiors filmed in France.

Hotel there was a note waiting for us from Cubby. He couldn't see us right away, but he'd meet us on Sunday at the Beverly Hills Hotel's Polo Lounge for lunch.

The ceremony was held at the Dorothy Chandler Pavilion on 3 April. Ken joined us, along with Cubby and Dana's daughters Tina and Barbara. The crowd outside seemed to go wild on our arrival, and as we went in Ken asked Tina, "Do you think they're cheering for us?" Looking over her shoulder, Tina pointed out that it was more likely they were pleased to see John Travolta, who was right behind us.

We didn't win that night – the art direction Oscar went to *Star Wars* – but we had a great time. After the ceremony Derek and I went to the party at the Beverly Hills Hilton, where I was delighted to meet the Hollywood star Macdonald Carey.

While we were in California we went to John Dykstra's workshop at Industrial Light & Magic, the special effects company established by George Lucas to make *Star Wars*. John showed me the model of the Imperial Star Destroyer that flew into shot at the beginning of that film. The ship looked vast on screen, so I was surprised to see that the model was only seven feet long.

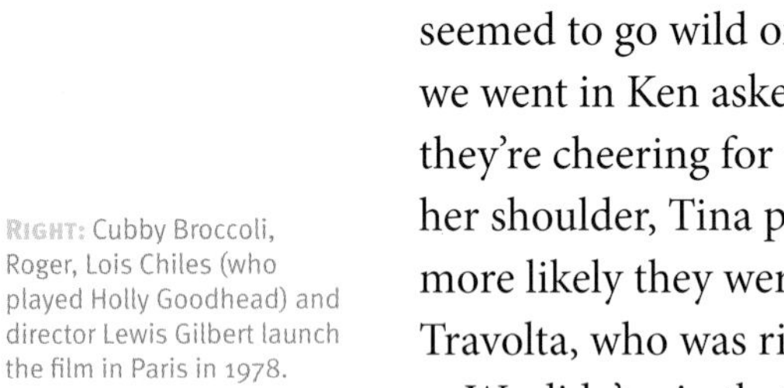

Right: Cubby Broccoli, Roger, Lois Chiles (who played Holly Goodhead) and director Lewis Gilbert launch the film in Paris in 1978.

Far right: A foreground miniature on the 007 Stage at Pinewood. The people and props were actually in the background and helped to create the illusion of size.

Below: Dr Goodhead, Bond and Jaws (Richard Kiel) in a scene filmed at Epinay, north of Paris. Ken's set was the biggest that had ever been constructed in a French studio.

Later on that trip we visited Palmdale, where NASA were preparing *Columbia*, the first Space Shuttle, for its anticipated launch the following year. Derek, Robin, my cousin Alan Maley and I arrived at the hangar in the back of a stretch limo. As we got out of the car we were greeted by a NASA official who assured us that while the project was on schedule, we mustn't interrupt or otherwise delay the contractors who were busy on the underside of the ship. Of course lots of these people immediately downed tools to come and look at our stupid car, which I thought was a little ironic given that we'd come all that way to look at the world's first reusable spacecraft!

On our way back to Los Angeles we went to see a guy in the San Fernando Valley who had a collection of snakes, spiders and other exotic animals. We were looking for a snake for the sequence where Bond (Roger Moore) has a close encounter with an underwater pet owned by the villain Hugo Drax (Michel Lonsdale). Our original intention was to find a tame anaconda, but the guy didn't keep any of them – possibly because they were too big. He offered us a python instead. "How big is it?" I asked. "About 30 feet long," he replied. This I had to see. It took about ten people to manhandle this thing over to us. Without getting too close, we knew we'd found our snake. It was eventually taken over to Florida, where the underwater shots were filmed and later combined with footage shot at one of the studios outside Paris.

Our final appointment in Los Angeles was with Art Karlson, the guy who ran the Glastron powerboat company. Glastron had supplied numerous boats for the bayou chase sequences in *Live and Let Die*, and would provide a load more for *Moonraker*, including the dark grey model driven by Bond.

Drax's operation was hidden behind the ancient Mayan ruins of Tikal in Guatemala, and this was the next location we visited. Along with Lewis, Ken, Derek, the associate producer Bill Cartlidge and other members of the crew we flew from Miami to Tikal aboard two small planes. Looking out of the window I saw nothing but dense trees for mile after mile until we suddenly flew over a clearing and this magnificent pyramid appeared out of nowhere. I'd brought a camera to take background plates – large images used in matte shots – and once I finished my survey I went to find the others. I discovered Derek seemingly transfixed by a tree. As I got closer I could see he was staring at an army of soldier ants marching up the trunk and through a hole in its side.

We returned to Guatemala City in a rainstorm that left us drenched. We were trudging back to our rooms looking like drowned rats when Ken appeared, telling us to get changed quickly because

Above left: The Mayan ruins at Tikal in Guatemala.

Above centre: Some of the model mountains that were placed in the foreground as the Space Shuttle launched.

Above right: This shot of a beach was also taken for the Shuttle take-off sequences.

Below left: Bond's boat was a Carlson Glastron CV23. It's pictured here on location in Florida, although the setting for this sequence was the Iguazu Falls in Brazil.

Right and far right: The cable cars at Sugarloaf Mountain in Brazil. We replicated these at Pinewood for close-ups of the fight between Bond and Jaws.

Below left: Derek's model of Drax's factory.

Below right: The same model on a rostrum at the Pinewood backlot.

we were going for dinner in an amazing place. When we convened downstairs we realised we were all wearing exactly the same type of jacket – it must have looked like an outing by the Dolly Sisters. Ken's amazing place turned out to be a restaurant serving a mountain of meat. Whichever piece you chose it was like chewing shoe leather.

Our next stop was Brazil, and this time we were flying economy. Ken got quite het up about this, so Lewis decided to wind him up. "I'm sorry Ken," he told him. "There were some places in first class but me and Peter got the last two..." He soon put Ken out of his misery by admitting it wasn't true.

At Rio we checked in at the beautiful Copacabana Palace, before looking at the cable cars where Bond would fight with Jaws (Richard Kiel) – back by popular demand after *The Spy Who Loved Me*. Our whistle-stop tour moved on to the Iguazu

Falls, where a powerboat chase would see Bond escaping in a hang glider while Jaws plunged over the edge. By this time, our group had been joined by Cubby's stepson, Michael G Wilson. Michael had been around on the Bond films in various capacities since *Goldfinger*, notably coming up with the idea for the breathtaking ski-parachute jump that opened *The Spy Who Loved Me*. For *Moonraker* he would be promoted to executive producer, and we were glad to have him along.

Ken's distress continued when we went to Paraguay, where he discovered that the box of Montecristo cigars he'd bought at the duty-free shop were all mouldy. We didn't even shoot anything there in the end.

From South America we went to Venice, where we found the shop the glassworks was based on and where Bond's motorised gondola had to rise out of the canal and drive across St Mark's Square. We bought two gondolas and sent them back to England to be customised by a special effects technician called John Evans. One of them was engineered to rise out of the water – which it eventually

ALBERT R. BROCCOLI presents
ROGER MOORE
as
JAMES BOND 007
in IAN FLEMING'S
"MOONRAKER"
Directed by LEWIS GILBERT

Telephone:
Iver: 651700.
Ext. No: 372.

From: Pinewood Film Studios,
IVER HEATH, Bucks...

Thursday, 12th April, 1979.

P.C.L. Facilities,
15, Pinewood Green,
IVER HEATH,
Bucks.
(Tel: Iver 654254)

Dear Sirs,

"M O O N R A K E R"

This letter confirms that, by mutual consent, we are extending Mr. Peter Lamont's employment with this Company by one week. His date of termination, therefore, will now be Friday, 27th April, 1979.

Yours faithfully,
For: EON PRODUCTIONS, LIMITED.

TERENCE CHURCHER.
Production Manager.

Les Productions Artistes Associés, 25-27 rue d'Astorg 75008 PARIS, FRANCE. Tel. (1) 265 4590, Cables UNARTISCO PARIS, Telex 650292
(Société Anonyme au Capital de 400 000 francs – R.C. PARIS 63 B 4387 SIRET: 632.043.873.00017 – CODE APE 8602 – INSEE: 871.75.908.0010)
Studios de Boulogne, 2, rue de Silly 92100 BOULOGNE, FRANCE tel. (1) 605 6569 Telex 270 061 Studios BLGSN
Eon Productions Ltd., 2 South Audley St., London W1Y 5DQ, England. Tel: (01) 493 7953. Cables: BROCFILM LONDON W1. Telex: 24351.
Pinewood Studios, Pinewood Road, Iver, Bucks, SL0 0NH, England. Tel: Iver (0753) 651 700. Cables: PINEWOOD IVER HEATH. Telex: 847505.

United Artists
A Transamerica Company

Above left: Jaws demonstrates the strength of his steel teeth in the cable car winding room.

Above right: Even letters to crew members were printed on this decorative *Moonraker* paper.

Left: Bond's hovercraft gondola glides through St Mark's Square.

Right: Cubby used to refer to Drax's control room as "the wigwam set".

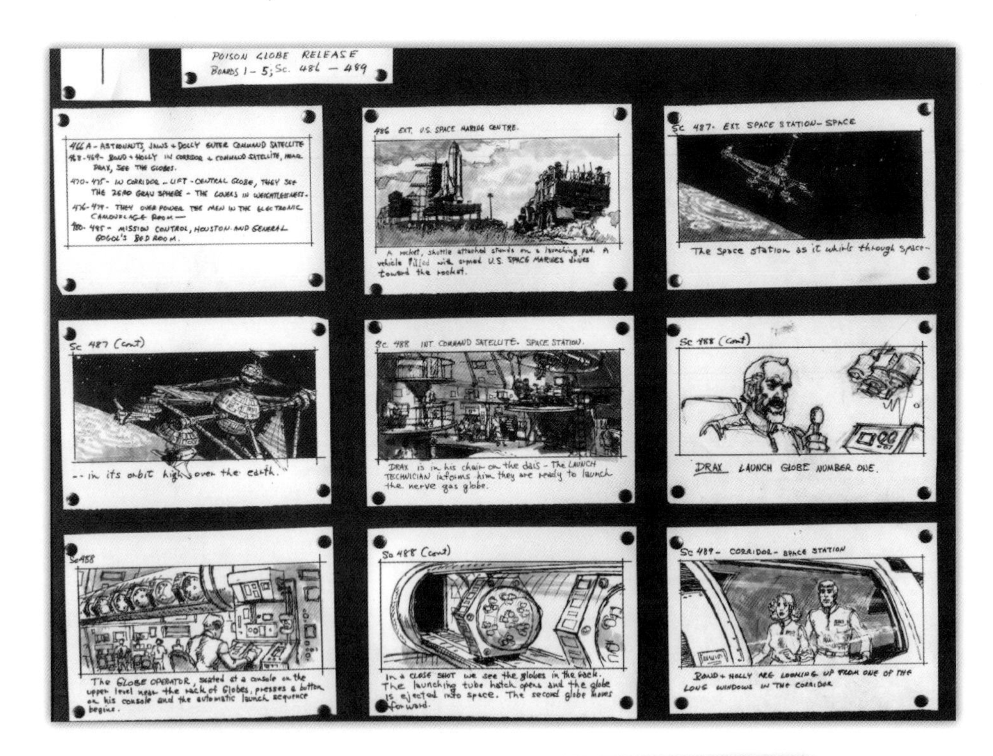

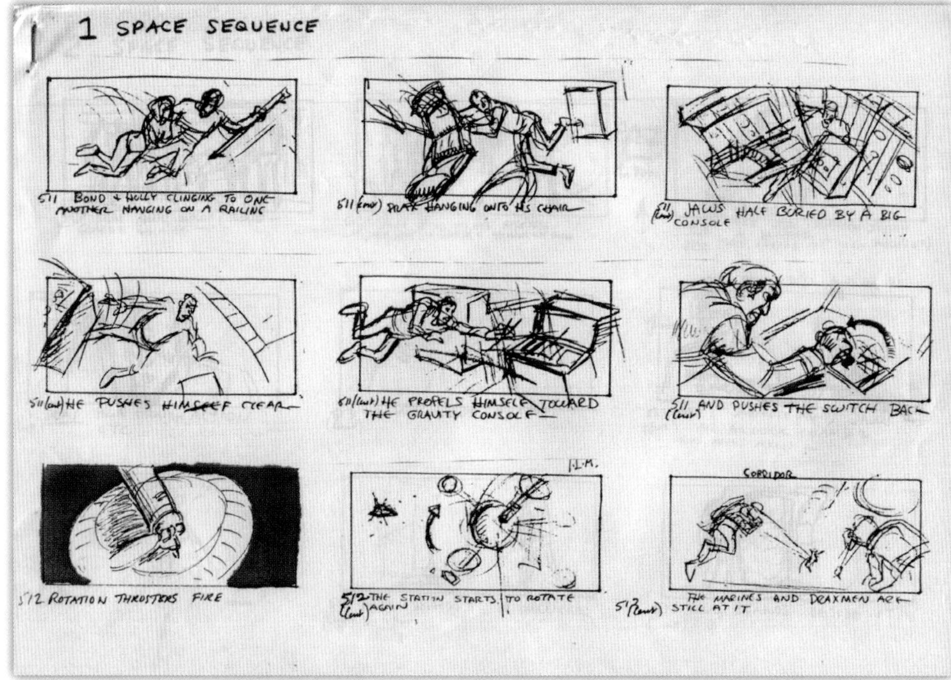

Top left and right: Storyboards for some of the special effects sequences we shot at Pinewood.

Above: Cameraman John Morgan films Jaws' view of the rapidly approaching circus tent for the pre-titles sequence.

managed to do after something like five attempts – and the other drove away, thanks to a mini that John managed to hide beneath its inflatable base.

After these location reconnaissance trips Charlie Bishop and a French art director called Max Duoy looked after things in Paris while I remained at Pinewood with Derek. Certain cable-car scenes and the exterior of Drax's space station were shot here, with the latter built on the 007 Stage. The illusion of deep space was created by draping the entire stage in a vast backdrop of black velvet. We reproduced the cargo hold of a Space Shuttle at full size to bring in the astronauts for the battle sequence at the end, later dropping them into the action from a runway built across the top of the stage.

Principal photography ran from August 1978 to February 1979, and during that time I made quite a few trips to Paris. The unions were much stricter than they were in the UK – three different studios were being used, but it wasn't permitted to share crew members between any of them, which effectively meant hiring three different crews. They worked unusual hours, from midday to eight o'clock during the week, and they were on double time if they had to work weekends.

Some of their working methods left me baffled – for example they refused to use metal scaffolding, instead building everything out of wood. They even tried to take a load of plywood to Brazil. We must have brought 20 forests' worth for them, and I never found out where it went after they finshed. They didn't use plaster either, so we had to take our own plasterers out there to build the swimming pool where Bond is attacked by the python.

Left and far left: Space marines disembark from the Shuttles and the laser battle begins.

Below right: My ticket to the royal premiere of *Moonraker* in June 1979.

Below left: I was given this commemorative belt buckle when filming was over.

Our plasterers worked over a weekend, for which the French crew charged double time before asking for two days off.

Moving production to France presumably saved a tax bill for some people, but in terms of the overall production I don't think it made any sense. And it certainly didn't help the budget, which Cubby told me ended up at $36 million. At one point I remember Andy Albeck, the president of United Artists, came out and there was a huge row about money. He was already nervous about the projected cost of Michael Cimino's western *Heaven's Gate* and he wasn't the only one with concerns over what had been spent on the sets for *Moonraker*.

Cubby didn't hold Ken entirely responsible for *Moonraker* going over-budget, but nevertheless this would prove to be Ken's final Bond film. He bowed out in spectacular style, as *The Spy Who Loved Me* and *Moonraker* feature some of his most stylish and opulent designs. I don't know whether Ken intended to draw a line under his Bond career at that time, but he went to Hollywood to work on the film adaptation of *Pennies from Heaven* (1982) and never came back.

NASA's Space Shuttle launch was delayed for two years, but this didn't seem to hurt *Moonraker* when it was released in June 1979. Some of the reviews were critical of the film's absurdities and jokey tone, but it grossed over $200 million around the world.

It was hard to imagine anything topping *Moonraker*'s laser battle in space, so it was decided not to try. For the sake of the narrative – and the budget – the next film in the series would adopt a back-to-basics approach.

LOTUS
turbo
esprit
GOODYEAR

FOR YOUR EYES ONLY

In the 1970s I had maintained a career parallel to the James Bond films, and when things were getting difficult with Ken Adam I was glad of the change of scenery.

When Ken lambasted me over the Bahamas shoot on *The Spy Who Loved Me* he was so furious he almost reduced me to tears. Feeling very despondent, I headed back to my office. In the corridor I was intercepted by the producer Stanley O'Toole. "Just the man I wanted to see!" he said, perking me up immediately. He shepherded me towards D Block, where the director Franklin J Schaffner offered me a job as art director on *The Boys from Brazil* (1978). Two years later, when I was free of my commitments on *Moonraker*, I went back to Stan and Frank to become the art director on their thriller *Sphinx* (1981).

The Egyptian location shoot for *Sphinx* finished in 1980. I had been at home for less than a day when the phone rang. It was Reg Barkshire, Eon's production controller. *For Your Eyes Only* was back on the schedule and they needed to find a new production designer. "So who would you like to work for?" asked Reg. I paused for a moment before plucking up the courage to ask, "Why don't you hire *me* as the production designer?" Reg said he'd call me back.

I knew everyone on the team, and after nine Bond films I certainly felt I knew the ropes. But I had a few anxious moments, wondering whether I'd done the right thing. Fifteen minutes later the phone rang again. It was Reg – I had the job. I don't know what happened during those 15 minutes, but I'm sure there was a discussion between Cubby and John Glen, who had just been promoted to director. I had first worked with John when he directed the second unit for *On Her Majesty's Secret Service* in Switzerland. He went on to edit that film, returning to handle the second unit and the editing of *The Spy Who Loved Me* and *Moonraker*, so we knew each other well.

Reg asked me to come to Eon's office in Mayfair. John was waiting for me when I got there, and together we went to see our producer. Cubby told us that the films were going to change direction. Though *The Spy Who Loved Me* and *Moonraker* had both been very successful, the character of Bond had to return to something closer to Ian Fleming's original vision. In the next film Bond would not be over-burdened with gadgets and he would become more central to the plot, detecting his way to the solution. The jokes and the

OPPOSITE PAGE: Roger Moore as James Bond, on location in Cortina with one of the Lotus Esprits.

TOP AND ABOVE: At Stoke Poges to film the opening sequence, where Bond visits his wife's grave and receives a message from the local vicar (Fred Bryant).

BELOW LEFT: I pinned my sketches of the film's interior sets to the art department wall.

BELOW RIGHT: Dana Broccoli took this picture of me, executive producer Michael G Wilson, Cubby and director John Glen at the Acropolis during our reconnaissance in Greece.

gadgets weren't the only things that were being reined in. The recent excesses were unsustainable – the budget for the new film would be $21 million, around a third less than that of *Moonraker*.

As well as John and me, Tom Pevsner came in as the associate producer and Anthony Waye joined as the assistant director. Cubby's reinvention of the Bond films was going to be carried out by a new team.

As production designer I had the privilege of choosing who I wanted to work with, so I asked John Fenner to be my art director. John had been around for a long time, and had worked his way up through the studios after starting his career in the print room, copying drawings for the art department. He'd been a draughtsman or assistant art director on the last four Bond films and I knew he was really talented. There were other familiar faces in the team, including my brother Michael, Ernie Archer and Don Picton as assistant art directors, Ronnie Quelch as the buyer and Michael Redding as construction manager.

One of the newcomers was junior draughtsman Crispian Sallis, son of the actor Peter Sallis. Crispian had worked with me on *Sphinx*, and before that he'd been a draughtsman on *Nijinsky* (1980), one of only two films Harry Saltzman had produced since leaving Eon. A novice member of the team was my son Neil, who had taken a close interest in my work ever since I'd brought him onto the volcano set of *You Only Live Twice* when he was six years old. Neil wanted to follow the family profession, so I gave him his first break by employing him as a gofer. Wary that I'd be accused of nepotism, I made sure he worked hard for the privilege.

Although I was now head of the art department, it didn't really change the way I worked. I did a few sketches on *For Your Eyes Only*, no more than usual, and I was perfectly happy for other people to do

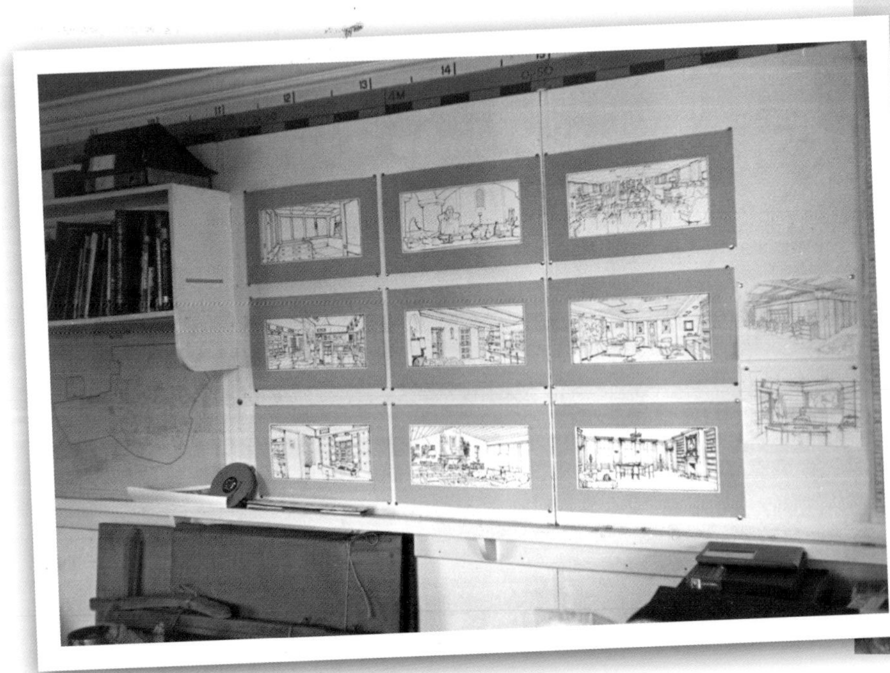

Clockwise from top left: Corfu was central to the film's location shoot; Melina's Citroën 2CV was souped up for the chase through the olive groves; we filmed the beach bungalow on the coast of Corfu; Willy Bogner's team of skiers joined us in the mountains near Cortina.

Below: I designed the ATAC computer and the prop was built by Don Fagan.

them. As a general rule, I think directors are more interested in being shown a model than a flat illustration. This enables them to see inside a scale representation of the set, giving them a much better idea of where they can put the actors and the cameras.

For Your Eyes Only was conceived as a 'low-tech' Bond film, at least in comparison to *Moonraker*, but at the heart of the story was the Automatic Targeting Attack Communicator – a handheld computer used by the Royal Navy's nuclear submarines. I had to dream up the design, because there was nothing like the ATAC in everyday life. There were rudimentary personal computers but there were certainly no laptops and this particular device had to be small enough for Bond (Roger Moore) to throw off the side of a cliff at the end of the film.

The rest of the film was no less challenging than *Moonraker*, even though we were working to a reduced budget. The script, by Richard Maibaum and Michael G Wilson, featured sequences on the sea, under the sea, in the air and up mountains, along with some complex chases in cars, on skis and on motorbikes. You name it, we were going to do it.

We started our search for locations by going to Athens. I went with Cubby, his wife Dana, John, Michael and the associate producer Tom Pevsner. Cubby and Dana then had to go back to England for personal reasons, while we continued south to Delphi. Here we photographed the ancient ruins as reference for the underwater temple that would appear in the film. We then went to Rome and Venice before splitting up. I looked at the ski resorts in Cortina and Innsbruck before going on to Munich. On a later trip we went to Corfu, where we found the beach, the olive groves, a village with a church and the bay where the Havelocks' boat was moored.

The boat was a yacht called *Thetis*, which we chartered in Cannes. It was chosen because it had a crane on its deck that we'd need to create the impression that a mini-submarine had been hoisted in and out of the water.

The ancient Greek temple where Melina (Carole Bouquet) and her colleagues conduct their archaeological research was due to be filmed underwater in Malta, in one of two tanks that had recently been used on *Raise the Titanic* (1980). We inspected these tanks, which were filled with sea water that had to be filtered and chlorinated because there was a sewage outlet nearby. Fish can't survive in chlorinated water, and of course we wanted exotic fish swimming in and out of the columns of our temple.

Our options were starting to look limited, until Michael suggested we went back to the Bahamas. Goulding Cay, a small island three miles west of Clifton Point, had been a mainstay of the Bond films ever since we shot *Thunderball* in the area more than 15 years earlier. The water was clear and exotic fish were abundant. Al Giddings, our underwater cameraman, was very experienced and very talented. We would trudge around with our cumbersome aqualungs while he would swim around like a dolphin. He would dive in with his snorkel, going right down to the sandbowl on the seabed, gliding around, going up and then right down again.

We wanted the temple to have a terrazzo floor which had to somehow be attached

Above: Sir Timothy Havelok (Jack Hedley) aboard his yacht.

Right: My original design for the interior of the Havelocks' yacht.

to the seabed. The design was made in the studio and then photographed by one of our stills men, Alan White. The images were then blown up, copied and encapsulated in Perspex. We also moulded the decaying sections of stone and remnants of ancient columns in blocks of fibreglass, which were shipped out to the Bahamas. Ken Court, one of my art directors, supervised putting everything in place underwater. I went out every other week to see how they were getting on. On one of these visits I learned there was a problem with the Perspex floor – it wouldn't stay put in its aluminium frame and was starting to flex with the motion of the water. On this occasion Cubby was also visiting, and he came up with an ingenious solution. He suggested we attached the Perspex to sheets of aluminium, which were then fixed to the frame. It solved the problem immediately.

Bond and Melina's exploration of the sunken *St Georges*, the British ship containing the ATAC, was also largely filmed in the Bahamas. Bond and Melina locate the wreck using the *Neptune*, the research submarine that usually sat on the deck of the Havelocks' yacht. I designed the prop, which was constructed from drawings that the draughtsman Jim Morahan made for me. Although this was a wet submarine I wanted it to look

Top left and centre: My brother Michael dressing the underwater set at Pinewood.

Above: The underwater temple is recreated in 60 feet of water at Goulding Cay in the Bahamas.

Left: Melina (Carole Bouquet) deposits her scuba gear at the temple in a shot from the film.

Far left: The *Thetis*, the yacht we chartered because it had a crane that could lift the *Neptune* research submarine.

Right: The fishing boat that doubled as the *St Georges*.

Far right: The *Neptune* was built as a full-size wet submarine and filmed in the Bahamas. A model of the submarine was subsequently shot in the tank at Pinewood.

Below left: A model of the *St Georges* is filmed at Pinewood Studios.

Below right: Bond and Melina approach the wreck of the *St Georges* aboard the *Neptune*, in these model shots from the film.

as authentic as possible, and this meant including a clear, dome-shaped nose for the front of the craft. A company in the South of France supplied just what we needed, moulded out of Plexiglass. While I was in the Bahamas, Tom and I went to Perry Oceanographics, the marine engineers I remembered from *The Spy Who Loved Me*. They fitted an engine to the *Neptune*, adding to the impression that it was a working submarine.

Prior to its destruction the *St Georges* was represented by a real fishing boat that we filmed off the coast of Great Yarmouth. For the undersea wreck, however, we used a model built by Derek Meddings and a large section of the hull with the side blown out. The script required Bond and Melina to talk to each other while they were looking for the ATAC inside the stricken ship. In *Thunderball* the divers had communicated with each other underwater by using a system of hand signals, but technology had moved on since the 1960s and I found a company in Yeovil that supplied communications devices that allowed us to hear what Bond and Melina were saying while they were in their diving suits.

The *Neptune* was due to be scrapped when filming in the Bahamas finished, but United Artists asked for it to be sent to America as part of their publicity campaign for the film. The submarine has now been restored by the dedicated fans at the Ian Fleming Foundation and still appears at exhibitions all over the world.

Lotus came up trumps with another white Esprit and a dummy which blew up when somebody tried to break into it. That particular scene was set in Spain, but we filmed all that in Corfu. When he loses his car, Bond has no choice but to get into Melina's Citroën 2CV. The car chase around those winding, mountainside roads was handled by Rémy Julienne and his stuntmen, who souped up the 2CV in preparation for its ordeal. Rémy was a lovely man and his team were great – to this day I've never seen driving like it.

LEFT: Rémy Julienne and his drivers shoot the car chase in Corfu.

BELOW: Bond wears a Seiko watch in the film.

RIGHT: Seiko made a small number of these commemorative watches for the crew. The 007 logo was engraved in gold on the back.

BOTTOM LEFT: General Gogol's office was adapted from Ken Adam's original design for the set in *The Spy Who Loved Me*.

BOTTOM RIGHT: My sketch of the interior of the ATAC room in the *St Georges*.

The skiing sequences were filmed in Cortina, a popular resort in Northern Italy. John and I had a repeat of the problems we'd faced while making *On Her Majesty's Secret Service* – the unusually mild weather meant we didn't have all the snow we needed, so we had to import it in trucks from elsewhere in the Dolomites. The ski chase was performed and partly filmed by an amazing man called Willy Bogner, who was someone else we'd worked with while making *On Her Majesty's Secret Service.*

My biggest challenge on *For Your Eyes Only* was St Cyril's, the abandoned monastery where the villain, Kristatos (Julian Glover), takes the stolen ATAC towards the end of the film. The Greek location was the Monastery of the Holy Trinity, built on top of a rock in Meteora. The monastery was designed to be impossible to attack when it was founded by Monk Dometios in 1438. More than 500 years later, when we went there on our reconnaissance, it was still virtually inaccessible. The top of the rock was more than 1,300 feet above ground, and unless you were an experienced mountaineer or a helicopter pilot the only way to gain entry was to climb a precarious ladder that led to a steep flight of steps carved inside.

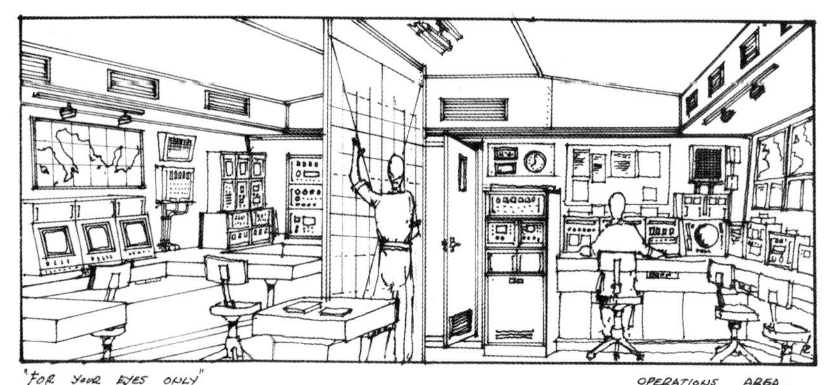

Right: A shot from the film showing the replica set we built on a plateau adjoining the real monastery at Meteora.

Below: A page from a brochure that I used to research my design for the replica monastery.

Far right: A publicity picture of Cubby, Sheena Easton (who sang the theme song), John Glen and Michael G Wilson.

THE HOLY MONASTERY OF ROUSSANOU

On a vertical single rock is perched the picturesque and peaceful Monastery of Roussanou. Most likely its name is owed to its first inhabitant, whose surname was Roussanos.

The official founders of the Monastery are two brothers from Ioannina, Maximos and Ioasaph, who in 1545 renovated and organized into a coenobion the already existing monastery. The rites established by the saintly founders are stated in their will, which is kept in the National Library of Athens (parchment scroll No 1465).

The main church is dedicated to the Transfiguration of the Savior and is illustrated by important frescos from 1561.

There is also a small chapel of Saint Barbara, where in the old days her Holy Skull was kept.

The Monastery of Roussanou, dilapidated with time, was recently restored by the Archaeological Survey, which has not completed its work as yet; therefore the monastery will remain closed for some time.

The most famous illustrations on the narthex are: the Death of Saint Nicolas and of Saint Efraim, a highly inspired work of art, the illustration of the Last Judgement and that of a scene in Paradise, where Adam names the different types of animals. The "Pantocrator" (Almighty) encircled by the angels, in the main hall, and the Extreme Humility, in the Sanctuary, are exceptional pictural creations.

3

The weather was terrible when we returned to Meteora to conduct our filming in mid-October 1980. Eon had made the necessary arrangements with the Orthodox Church in Athens, but it seems the message hadn't reached the monks, who were so unhappy at our presence that they put oil barrels on the roof and hung their laundry from the windows in an effort to spoil our shots. Things got so difficult that we built a dummy monastery and a helicopter pad on the adjoining rock, which fortunately was accessible by road. In the finished film the mountaineering scenes and Bond's final confrontation with General Gogol (Walter Gotell) were filmed on the neighbouring rock, with the original site relegated to carefully chosen long shots.

Even if the monks had been more co-operative, it would have been time-consuming and possibly dangerous to spend too long filming on top of the rock at Meteora. The interior of the monastery was recreated at Pinewood on a big composite set that took up most of B Stage.

Meteora was a difficult shoot, so when it was over I invited everyone on the crew for a meal at a local restaurant. There were about 20 of us, and when we finished I counted 29 empty wine bottles at the end of our table. The entire bill only came to £76!

The film premiered in London on 24 June 1981, and afterwards I reflected on what had been a very happy experience. I had got to know Michael much better during 1980, and during our location reconnaissance trips with him, Tom and John we all became mates. Michael is very laid back, very quiet and always listens to what you have to say. During one of our trips together I remember we were both on the back seat of a car when he reached into his bag and produced this strange little box and a couple of sets of headphones. He plugged one set of headphones into the box and handed me the other, which I also plugged in. He pressed a button and suddenly I could hear music. Michael had one of the first Sony Walkman players, and

I'd never seen anything like it. Fortunately we both shared the same taste in tunes!

I got on similarly well with John, and to this day we've never had a cross word. I'd worked with some terrible prima donnas on pictures but, like Michael, John is someone who will always listen to what you have to say. If I thought there was a better way of doing something then he'd usually give it a go.

For Your Eyes Only was John's first film as a director, but he was such an experienced editor that he knew exactly what to shoot and how to shoot it. A piece of advice I once received from the renowned Edward Carrick applies to directors as much as it applies to production designers: you have to design a set appropriate to the stage directions in a script. If the scene describes someone entering a room and being thrown out of a window, you'd better make sure your set has a door and window or your director's going to be in trouble. John understands what to shoot to make a sequence fit together in the edit, and takes exactly what he needs from the script. It's part of what makes him such an efficient director.

John, Michael and myself were all exploring new roles when we made *For Your Eyes Only*, and the success of the film meant we entered the new decade with a renewed sense of confidence.

FAR LEFT: Roger Moore and Carole Bouquet joking between takes in the keelhauling sequence. Filming began in Corfu and was intercut with underwater footage shot in the Bahamas.

LEFT AND ABOVE: My ticket to the premiere and a poster promoting the event.

011

OCTOPUSSY

In 1981 I was asked to head the art department of a big fantasy epic called *Ladyhawke*. I went to Czechoslovakia several times to find the locations, but didn't get much further before the whole production ground to a halt, I suspect because the producers realised the challenges of shooting in a country that was behind the Iron Curtain.

When Eon heard I was looking for another job they asked me not to, in case it overlapped with the next Bond film. To keep me busy in the meantime, Cubby asked me to help fix the sash windows at his office in Audley Square. By the time we'd finished redecorating it was time to begin work on *Octopussy*.

For Your Eyes Only had been deemed such a success that Roger Moore, John Glen and Tom Pevsner were also invited back. Like *For Your Eyes Only*, *Octopussy* was inspired by one of Ian Fleming's short stories, the stock of available novels now having been exhausted.

The commercial failure of *Heaven's Gate* had terrible consequences for United Artists in 1981, and by the time we began work on *Octopussy* the following year the company had been taken over by MGM. I understood that the decision to shoot *Octopussy* in India was at least partly prompted by MGM/UA, who had a source of production money tied up in the country.

On our first reconnaissance trip – which began in India – John, Tom and I were joined by Michael G Wilson. As well as being the executive producer, Michael would share the film's screenplay credit with the longstanding Dick Maibaum and the film's original writer, George MacDonald Fraser.

We arrived in Delhi and then spent a day driving to Jaipur, the capital of Rajasthan in Northern India. We stayed at the Rambagh Palace, a beautiful hotel with huge bathrooms, plush beds and big, roaring fires. India is well known for being a country of contrasts, and it felt strange to enjoy all this luxury while emaciated locals were herding cows through the streets.

We met Bhawani Singh, the Maharaja of Jaipur, at the City Palace. Nicknamed 'Bubbles' because of the amount of Champagne consumed to celebrate his birth, the Maharaja was keen to help the production of a James Bond film in any way he could.

On our way to the palace I had noticed an elderly beggar woman dressed in some of the worst rags I'd ever seen.

OPPOSITE PAGE: Executive producer Michael G Wilson, associate producer Tom Pevsner and producer Cubby Broccoli in the Kremlin war room – one of my favourites among the sets I designed for *Octopussy*.

TOP: Standing alongside Octupussy's ornate bed, which was designed by my art director John Fenner.

ABOVE: Assistant director Tony Waye, director John Glen, Michael G Wilson and director of photography Alan Hume, on location in India.

RIGHT AND FAR RIGHT: The helicopter delivering Bond to Udaipur gave us a spectacular view of the Taj Mahal along the way.

BELOW LEFT AND RIGHT: Two views of the Monsoon Palace. The exteriors of Kamal Khan's luxurious residence were shot in Udaipur and the interiors were created back at Pinewood.

I couldn't walk past without giving her some money. When I returned the next day I noticed she wasn't there. At the next street corner I saw a car pull by the side of the road. She got out of the car, changed into the rags and headed back to her usual spot. What an actress!

Our efforts to look around Jaipur were hampered by the fact that the local taxi drivers had chosen that week to go on strike. Rashid, our resourceful guide, told us not to worry, before disappearing down the road. He came back with a 50-seat bus that he'd somehow managed to procure at short notice. We climbed aboard and headed for the local lake. It was an interesting trip, but in the end we decided not to film at the lake or indeed anywhere in Jaipur.

The next day, we drove to Udaipur, another city in Rajasthan. It was here that we found the Taj Lake Palace in Lake Pichola, which became the home of Octopussy (Maud Adams). Overlooking the lake we found the Monsoon Palace, which became the home of our villain, Kamal Khan (Louis Jourdan). I spent as much time as I could looking at the inside of the palaces as well as the outside, as I didn't want to design anything that wasn't true to the place we were visiting. Ever since we'd faithfully recreated the inside of the Vulcan bomber in *Thunderball* I'd tried to ensure our interiors were as accurate as possible, and I maintained this philosophy in India.

The hotel Bond stayed at in the film was the Shiv Niwas Palace, on the banks of Lake Pichola. This was the former residence of the Maharana and was in the process of being adapted to a hotel when we were there. They were very keen for us to choose the hotel as a location, and as well as filming inside John used the garden for the elephant chase.

Rashid had promised that Udaipur would be spectacular and he didn't let us down – everything that George had written about was there. We couldn't have asked for anything better. Unfortunately the same couldn't be said for our accommodation that night. There were only two rooms available at the best hotel, so John and Michael stayed there. Tom and I gallantly volunteered to stay in a place at the end of the lake that shall remain

nameless. As I looked around my grotty room, dimly lit by a flickering fluorescent tube, I consoled myself with the fact that at least the sheets were clean.

We flew back to Delhi, and from there went to Katmandu, where I saw Everest on the horizon. We then visited the town of Maholi in Uttar Pradesh. Standing in the shadow of the mighty Himalayas was an awe-inspiring experience that I think made us all feel a bit insignificant. The next stop was Goa, but a planned visit to Madras was cancelled by Cubby, who was content that we'd seen enough.

Our reconnaissance trips were occasionally uncomfortable, sometimes arduous, but in August 1982 my next trip to Jaipur went beyond either of those descriptions. It was the one time I feared that location scouting for a Bond film might actually cost me my life.

By this time, Eon had a production office in Udaipur. I popped in to collect the air tickets for the rest of the crew to fly from London to India. I put the tickets in my bag and boarded the plane for Jaipur at the local airport. We made a stopover at Jodhpur, and shortly after the plane took off I noticed a flurry of movement ahead of us, between the toilet and the flight deck. A few minutes later the pilot switched on the intercom and announced, "Good morning ladies and gentlemen. We're not going to land at Jaipur because we've been hijacked. Our new destination is Lahore." I looked around at my fellow passengers, all of whom were in a state of shock.

As we approached Lahore I looked out of the window to see that we were expected. Lorries had been positioned along the runway, in an attempt to prevent us landing. The plane circled the airport for about an

Below left: My design of Bond's hotel room was inspired by decor I'd seen in the Shiv Niwas Palace Hotel in Udaipur. The set (pictured beneath) was constructed at Pinewood.

Below right: My sketch of the 'sleazy café' visited by Kamal Khan (Louis Jourdan, pictured beneath) included a detail showing how his henchman's swinging chainsaw could be operated from the balcony.

Below and bottom: The staircase and dining room of Kamal Khan's residence were parts of a huge composite set built at Pinewood. The set also included Bond's bedroom and parts of the palace exterior.

Bottom right: Cubby with the stuffed tiger we used to decorate the set.

hour, until our Sikh separatist hijacker forced the pilot to try to land anyway. He made his approach with the wheels down, but still the lorries didn't budge. He eventually pulled up and we flew away from the airport. We must have been running low on fuel by the time we landed in Amritsar. The plane taxied off the runway and came to a halt in one of the bays by the side of the airport. The engines fell silent.

The heat inside the aircraft cabin was stifling and everyone was drenched in sweat. Our hijacker appeared, and I could see he was armed with a hand grenade and a pistol. He opened the doors at the front and the rear of the plane to get some air flowing. Members of the Indian security forces gathered on the tarmac outside, with their fingers on their triggers.

Some of the female passengers weren't coping, so the hijacker allowed two of them and their children to get off. One man helped his wife to the front of the plane. Along the way he took the opportunity to discreetly hatch a plan with the pilot.

Everyone that remained was told to move to the rear of the plane, leaving our belongings. As I walked away from my bag the only thought in my head was that Iris Rose, our production assistant, would bloody kill me if I lost the crew's tickets!

The man who had helped his wife sat in one of the empty seats next to me. "So what do you do for a living?" he asked me. "I work for the people who make the James Bond films," I replied. "Right..." he said. "I don't suppose you've got any of those gadgets on you?" I shot him a withering look.

Some of us got up, and the man started gesticulating to the pilot. The hijacker noticed something was going on and waved his gun around, but while he was distracted the pilot went back into the cockpit and grabbed a fire axe. Creeping up on the hijacker he brought the axe down on the back of his head. The guy dropped his grenade – fortunately with the pin still in place – and started firing shots into the cabin. We all dived to the floor as he grabbed the door frame in a vain attempt to regain his balance. The hijacker fell out of the door and we immediately heard the sound of sub-machine gun fire. The ensuing silence was broken by the sound of Indian soldiers clambering onto the plane with rifles and fixed bayonets.

We were told to leave the plane by sliding down the emergency chute that had inflated over the wing. One of the passengers was in such a hurry to get off that he grabbed his bag and jumped out of the front door, breaking his ankle. He was taken to hospital, while we were taken to a hotel and debriefed before being told we were free to go.

When I got back to England John was shooting the exteriors of Octopussy's circus at RAF Upper Heyford near Oxford. It was such a good-natured shoot that we even allowed the peace protestors camped outside the base to use our toilets. Other British locations included the Nene Valley Railway in Peterborough, which played host to Bond's escape from Karl-Marx-Stadt. This complemented footage of the real Checkpoint Charlie and other locations on the border between East and West Germany.

ABOVE LEFT AND RIGHT: My sketch of the war room, alongside a picture of the dressed set. The centre of the floor revolved, allowing the committee members to face a screen on the right-hand wall.

BELOW LEFT: Steven Berkoff (as General Orlov, on the rails), Walter Gotell (as General Gogol, centre) and John Glen, on location at the Nene Valley Railway in Peterborough.

Below left: Beautiful concept art of the jewelled egg by Maciek Piotrowski. The egg was designed in the style of Peter Carl Fabergé.

Below right: "I think this should be ample security..." Bond (Roger Moore) raises the stakes during a game of backgammon with Kamal Khan.

My team on *Octopussy* included a number of familiar faces, such as assistant art director Ernie Archer. Ernie and I went way back, and he was almost 20 years older than me. Perhaps this was why he always called me 'boy', even though I was his boss on this and *For Your Eyes Only*. Ernie was getting on but his talent was undimmed and there was magic in his drawings of the Monsoon Palace. These drawings, and George's notes, were the blueprint for a huge composite set that we built on Pinewood's A Stage. Fred Hole was another stalwart of the Eon art department, a great nuts-and-bolts guy who had created many of the mechanical props in the *You Only Live Twice* volcano. In *Octopussy*, Fred's props included the circus cannon and the atomic bomb.

The Fabergé Egg that Bond tricks Kamal into buying at Sotheby's was one of the film's most important props, and when John asked me to make the real and fake eggs I had to assure him they would be of the highest quality. Ronnie Quelch, who had helped me with the vanity cases for *On Her Majesty's Secret Service*, went back to Asprey in New Bond Street. Asprey made the eggs to our specifications, although the tiny state coaches inside were items they had in stock.

Sometimes functionality had to take precedence over opulence. Octopussy had four fish tanks in her room, including one that contained her pet octopus. Ernie did a beautiful job on the tanks and their stands, but I was concerned they would overpower the room. I expressed my doubts as soon as I saw them, but everybody said I'd be able to talk John into using them. I decided I wasn't going to talk John into anything – they were wrong, and as I'd approved them it was my fault. I turned to Ronnie and told him about an Italian company on the Fulham Road that made square table legs that clipped together. He went to see them and they made four bases for us. We had the tanks remade, put them on top and

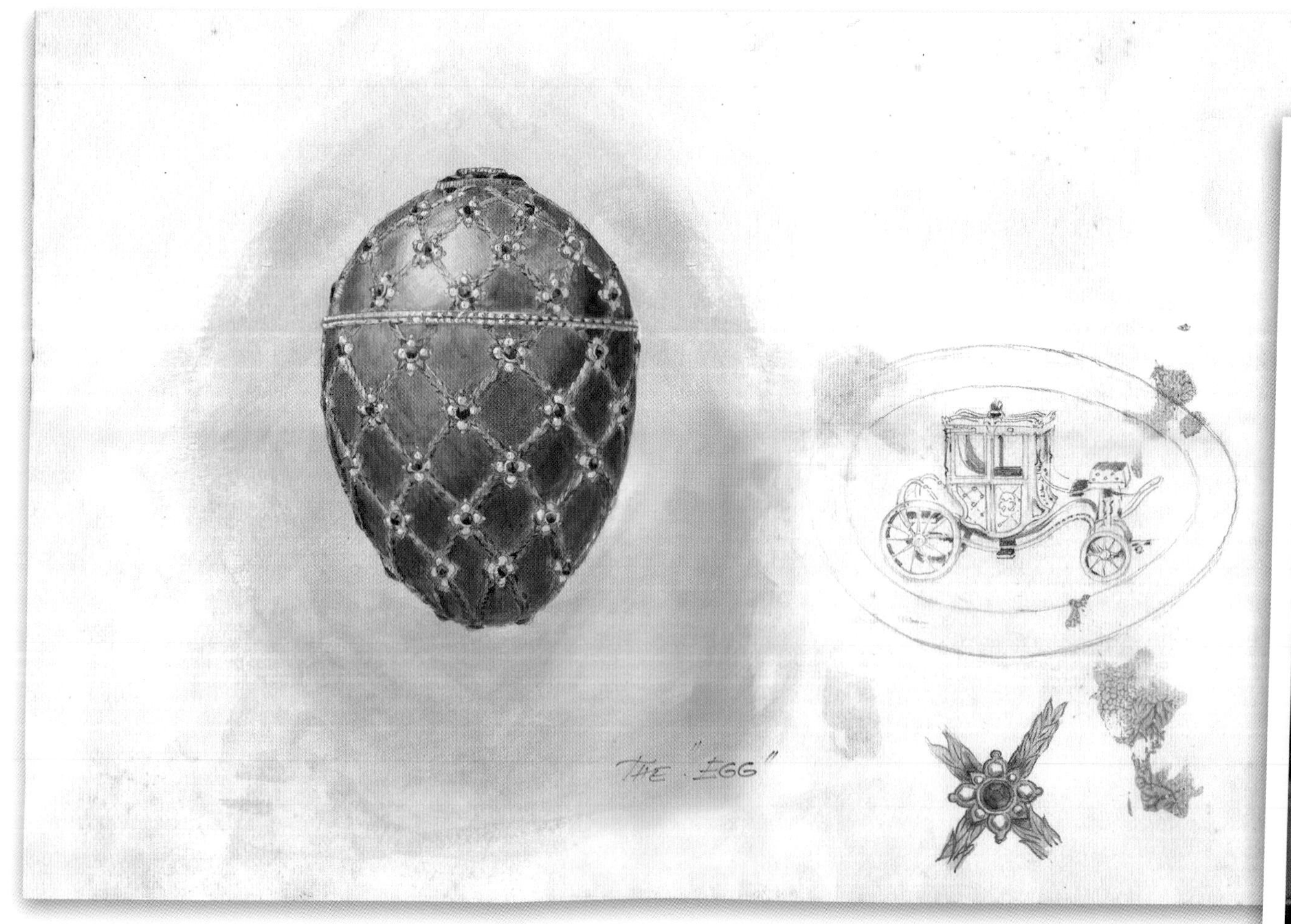

they looked just right. The design for Octopussy's ornate bed was by the art director John Fenner, who did a great job, and the Indian sets were dressed by Crispian Sallis with exemplary flair.

The film ends with a lingering shot of Octopussy's barge, beautifully shot at sunset by John's director of photography, Alan Hume. We'd found the barge on our second visit to Udaipur, when Rashid told us about two matching boats on the other side of Lake Pichola. We picked the best boat, renovating it with parts cannibalised from one of the others.

The Indian construction manager on the project was called Mr Dikshit – I'm not joking – and his labourers somehow hauled the boats up on two piles of bricks. I created a drawing of what I wanted the finished barge to look like and Mike Turk, our boatmaster, taught Octopussy's girls how to row.

We finished shooting in January 1983 and the film opened in June to excellent box-office returns, especially in America. Kevin McClory's long-mooted Bond film, a remake of *Thunderball* called *Never Say Never Again*, finally appeared in October. *Never Say Never Again* wasn't much discussed by any of us back then, even though it was being shot at Elstree at much the same time we were making *Octopussy* at Pinewood. It was wonderful to see Sean Connery back in the role of Bond, but the rest of the film was strikingly different to those that had been produced by Eon over the last 20 years. Our team had spent decades establishing an inimitable style that couldn't be equalled.

LEFT: My sketch of Octopussy's ceremonial barge.

BELOW LEFT AND CENTRE: Two shots of the renovated boat, as it appeared in the film.

BELOW RIGHT: A publicity flyer for *Octopussy*, which was released in June 1983.

ZORIN
INDUSTRIES

A VIEW TO A KILL

While I was working as the production designer of *Top Secret!*, a comedy directed by Jim Abrahams and David Zucker, Eon and MGM/UA were negotiating with Roger Moore to star in his seventh James Bond film. The success of *Octopussy* made Roger the favourite to play 007 again, despite his advancing years. He knew, however, that this would definitely be his final Bond movie.

A View to a Kill would reunite the team that had made *For Your Eyes Only* and *Octopussy*. John Glen was our director and I was once again happy to be working with John Fenner, Mickey Redding, Ronnie Quelch, Crispian Sallis and many others on my team.

The principal locations in Richard Maibaum and Michael G Wilson's script were France and the United States. I joined Michael, assistant director Barbara Broccoli, associate producer Tom Pevsner and John Glen on the first reconnaissance trip, which began at a stud farm at Le Touquet in northern France. We then drove to a restaurant outside Paris to see a remarkable act where a whistling lady on a stage appeared to control butterflies that hovered over the heads of the diners. Dominique Risbourg, the illusionist who owned the restaurant, agreed to recreate the act for us when we filmed Bond's meeting with the ill-fated Monsieur Aubergine (Jean Rougerie) at Pinewood.

The restaurant where Aubergine is murdered was the only part of the Eiffel Tower that we recreated at Pinewood – the rest was shot on the real thing. On another visit to France I visited the Tower, this time accompanied by director of photography Alan Hume and production supervisor Tony Waye. Tom Pevsner had an appointment to talk to the authorities, to get permission for May Day (in this instance played by stuntman BJ Worth) to parachute from a diving board discreetly placed at the top of the Tower.

While Tom was in the meeting he left me with the float and asked me to buy lunch for Alan, Tony, John and myself in the Gustave Eiffel Restaurant on the first floor. I noticed there were no prices on the menu, but decided to treat myself anyway. Tom returned before the meal was over so I handed the float back to him. When the bill arrived his eyes widened. "What idiot had caviar blinis?" he asked. "I did," I confessed. "That cost more than everyone else's meals put together!" he replied.

OPPOSITE PAGE: The quarter-size airship and quarter-size tower of the Golden Gate Bridge on the Pinewood backlot. These models were built by special effects supervisor John Richardson.

TOP: Dressed for Ascot at the art department's Christmas party in 1984. From left to right – Tony Rimmington, me, Johnny Chisolm, John Fenner, Stan Giles and Mike Boon.

ABOVE: Bond (Roger Moore) pursues May Day at the Eiffel Tower.

Right and far right: Two of my sketches of the Eiffel Tower restaurant where Bond meets Aubergine.

Below right and far right: The Pinewood set, as it appeared in the film.

Bottom right: Scaling the Eiffel Tower with colleagues from the art department.

That afternoon, John, Tom and I flew down to Nice for the next leg of the recce. Michael was waiting for us at the airport when we arrived. "We're all staying at the Negresco Hotel," he told us, before innocently adding, "I hear the caviar blinis are sensational!"

Bond's investigation takes him from Paris to San Francisco, where Max Zorin (Christopher Walken) plans to flood Silicon Valley, giving him and his associates dominance of the world's microchip production. For one of our trips to San Francisco, Michael, Barbara, Tom, John and I were accompanied by Arthur Wooster, the second unit director. We chartered a helicopter which flew us under the Bay Bridge before taking us over the Golden Gate. This would be the location for the climactic fight between Bond and Zorin, and we got a good idea of how this would look from the air. We then flew over the San Andreas Fault, the tectonic boundary that Zorin planned to disrupt to trigger the flood.

Back in San Francisco we visited Japantown, Fisherman's Wharf and Alcatraz, before Tom and I crossed the Bay to Oakland, visiting the grand property we hoped to use as the house belonging to geologist Stacey Sutton (Tanya Roberts). After the others returned to London, Tom and I stayed on in San Francisco to negotiate with

the owner of the house. He was initially reluctant to hire the place to us, but we eventually persuaded him. Sometime later I discovered that the place had previously been used as the location for a porn movie set in a girls' school and that all sorts had gone on there – possibly giving the owner cause to be mistrustful of filmmakers!

Our trip to California also included some research into the scientific and technological aspects of Zorin's operation. We went to Stanford University and a research laboratory in Berkeley, on the eastern shore of the Bay, where we saw a beta particle accelerator in action. The two-mile tunnel where scientists were bombarding the particles was built across the San Andreas Fault. Back in the UK we went to the Inmos factory in Newport, Wales, to see microprocessors being manufactured, and visited the Renault plant in Swindon, which would become the location for Zorin's warehouse.

Principal photography was due to start at Pinewood in summer 1984, but the schedule was jeopardised by a disaster that occurred on a completely different film on 27 June. I was in A Block, working in my office, when I noticed a cloud of smoke outside the window. Moments later it was accompanied by the smell of burning. At first I thought somebody must have lit a bonfire, but I thought I'd better go outside to check. Walking towards the plume of smoke, I soon realised that the 007 Stage was on fire. The heat from the blaze had melted the steel holding up the walls and roof, leaving a buckled mass of twisted metal in a huge heap on the ground. The fire brigade were training their hoses on something that already resembled the wreck of the *Hindenburg*.

ABOVE LEFT: The 007 Stage on fire in June 1984.

ABOVE RIGHT: Celebrating Stan Giles' birthday at Pinewood.

FAR LEFT: May Day (here played by BJ Worth) jumps from the top of the Eiffel Tower.

LEFT: Stacey Sutton's house was filmed on location in Oakland, California.

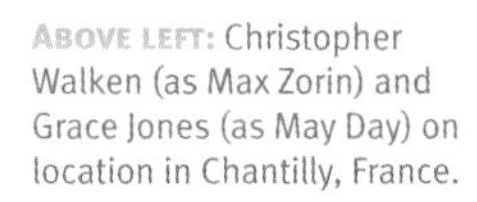

Above left: Christopher Walken (as Max Zorin) and Grace Jones (as May Day) on location in Chantilly, France.

Top right: Ascot Racecourse was another of the film's glamorous locations.

Above right: Chateau Chantilly, north of Paris, was the location for Zorin's French residence.

The stage was being used for the Ridley Scott film *Legend*, and rumour has it the fire was triggered by some boiling paraffin wax that had been left unattended. The blaze had started during a lunch break, which at least meant that none of the cast or crew was around to get hurt.

Ridley shifted the final weeks of the forest scenes for *Legend* to a location and another soundstage, but our production would need a more drastic rethink. I had planned to build the interior of Zorin's mine as a huge, composite set that could be flooded with water from the tank inside the 007 Stage.

Tom Pevsner was also looking for a solution and told me that Elstree Studios had offered us the use of their Stage 6. Commonly known as the *Star Wars* Stage, because it had been specially built for *The Empire Strikes Back* in 1979, this enormous building boasted 30,000 square feet. It was a tempting offer, until I discovered that Elstree wouldn't allow us to take any of our existing staff from Pinewood.

Michael Brown, the architect who had drawn up the plans for the original 007 Stage, told me that once the debris was removed it would take 13 weeks to build something new. I shared this information with Cyril Howard, Pinewood's managing director, before making an appointment to see Cubby. He was in an understandably sombre mood as I explained the options to him. "So it comes down to this," I concluded. "Do you or don't you want to rebuild the 007 Stage?"

He didn't hesitate for a moment. "I want to rebuild it." The decision was made, and it was actioned that day.

Michael Brown's team of builders moved in as soon as the site was cleared. Unfortunately it proved impossible to stick to his estimated schedule because the tank needed to be realigned – the natural springs beneath Pinewood had given us a valuable source of water while *The Spy Who Loved Me* was shooting during the drought of 1976, but they had left a void underneath the stage that now needed to be filled.

The new stage would still be classed as a temporary structure for the purposes of planning permission, but its construction gave me the opportunity to fix something that had been niggling me about the original ever since it had been built. There was a kind of drop around the edges of the floor, so we filled this in with concrete. This gave us more floor space than we'd ever had before.

Another issue had become apparent more recently, and we were able to fix that too. When we built the exterior of Octopussy's palace on the stage we installed a huge cyclorama behind it. When I'd check the set in the mornings I'd often notice a big black line running all the way round this backing. This was damp, caused by condensation that ran down from the roof. It would disappear as soon as the studio lights warmed things up, but this was something that had to be dealt with. For the new stage we installed a double-skinned roof to help tackle the problem.

All the time the stage was being built, and the health and safety people were making their checks, I was thinking about how quickly we could erect the mine set. The area needed to be flooded, and because there was no way to trick the scale of the flowing water the set had to be huge. I'd shipped components of it onto other stages at Pinewood while we were waiting, and we'd flooded two of them already, but there came a point when we really couldn't go any further without moving everything onto the 007 Stage.

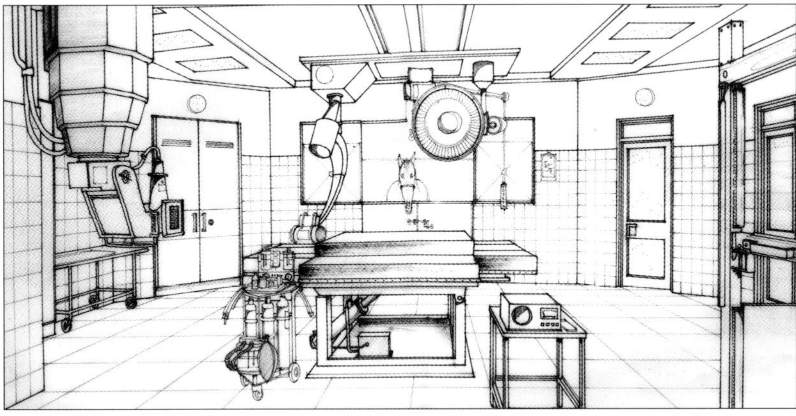

FAR LEFT: My sketch of the equine surgery and the set (pictured beneath) as it appeared in the film.

LEFT: The interior of the Zorin airship gondola. In the picture beneath, Zorin addresses his prospective associates on the set we built at Pinewood.

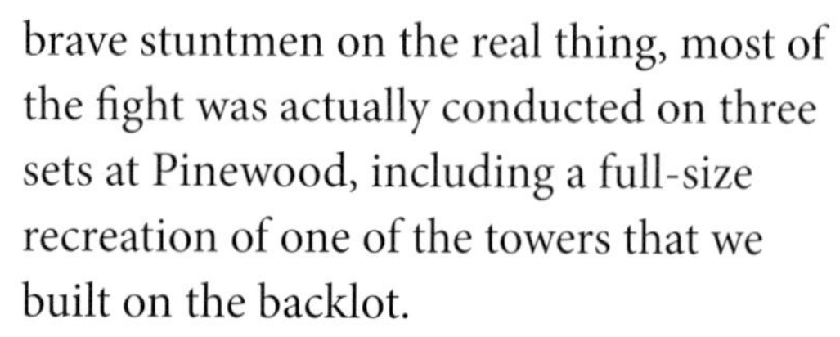

Above left: Fiona Fullerton, Roger Moore, Cubby Broccoli, Tanya Roberts, Christopher Walken and Alison Doody at the official re-opening of the 007 Stage on 7 January 1985.

Above right: Roger, Fiona and Christopher inside the stage on the same day.

Far right: The quarter-size airship and Golden Gate tower on the Pinewood backlot.

Below: The elaborate mine set we constructed on the new 007 Stage.

Everything was finally ready at the end of 1984 and we started shooting after Christmas. The new facility was named 'The Albert R Broccoli 007 Stage' and officially opened by Cyril Howard and MGM/UA's Frank E Rosenfelt on 7 January 1985, the week after we'd finished filming.

The entrance of the mine was supposed to be in California but was filmed at Amberley in West Sussex, at a 36-acre working museum housed in a former chalk pit. The Zorin Industries shed outside the mine entrance was a set we constructed, but the airship that emerged from it when Zorin left the site was real. My brother Michael had to go RAF Cardington to get the airship, and we then had to cover up the large advertisement for Fuji that appeared on its side.

The airship's final destination in the film was the Golden Gate Bridge. Front projection, supervised by Charlie Staffell at Pinewood, helped to create the impression that Christopher Walken and Roger Moore were slugging it out on top of the bridge. Apart from some scenes filmed by very brave stuntmen on the real thing, most of the fight was actually conducted on three sets at Pinewood, including a full-size recreation of one of the towers that we built on the backlot.

The plates for the front projection had been filmed during one of our trips to the bridge, when Tom had secured permission for us to go to the top of the North Tower.

I was the first one up there, along with two armed guards, squashed into a tiny lift that was normally only used for maintenance purposes. When the lift came to a halt I climbed some steps and emerged through a hatch at the top. The view that greeted me was breathtaking – there was a panoramic view of San Francisco Bay to one side, the Pacific Ocean to the other, and a 750-foot drop beneath me. Eventually I was joined by Michael, Tom, special effects supervisor John Richardson and John Glen as we took photographs and made measurements.

At one point somebody casually strolled up one of the giant cables suspending the bridge and asked us what we were doing. He was a painter, curious about the sudden flurry of activity. I said, "We're making a film." Satisfied with the response, he turned around and nonchalantly headed back down the cable.

From the parachute jump off the Eiffel Tower to the flooding of the mine, *A View to a Kill* is full of set-pieces that nowadays would probably be created, or at least fixed, in post-production using computer-generated images. This technology wasn't available to us in 1985, but you couldn't miss what you'd never had. Although there were matte shots, front projection and an army of stuntmen doubling for Roger on his farewell performance, here was a film where we tried to create as much of the action 'in camera' as possible. It's a philosophy we upheld during my entire tenure on the James Bond films.

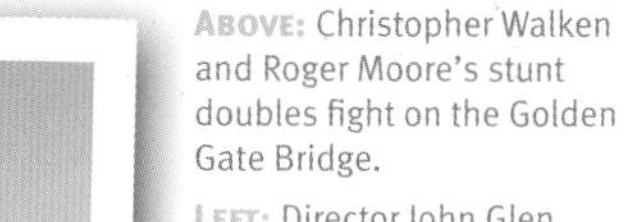

Above: Christopher Walken and Roger Moore's stunt doubles fight on the Golden Gate Bridge.

Left: Director John Glen during our reconnaissance trip to the North Tower.

Bottom left: Production accountant Douglas Noakes, John Richardson and me after the British premiere on 12 June 1985.

Bottom right: With Grace Jones at the film's wrap party on Pinewood's A Stage.

THE LIVING DAYLIGHTS

In 1985 a meeting with a young American director changed the course of my career. James Cameron asked me to be the production designer of *Aliens*, a sequel he was conceiving in a very different style to the first film in the series, Ridley Scott's *Alien* (1979). *Aliens* was essentially a science-fiction war film, shot at Pinewood and on location in Acton on a budget of around $18 million. The film would bring me BAFTA and Oscar nominations (the latter alongside set decorator Crispian Sallis) and began a long and happy association with Jim that would lead to even greater things in the 1990s.

My commitment to Cubby Broccoli and Eon's James Bond films never wavered, however, and in 1986 I began work on *The Living Daylights*, the first film in the series to star Timothy Dalton. Director John Glen would prove his versatility by introducing a harder, more serious tone to complement Timothy's portrayal of the character. John Fenner wasn't available to be art director on this one, so I asked Terry Ackland-Snow to take his place. Terry and I had been draughtsmen together in the 1960s and he'd been my supervising art director on *Aliens*.

Cubby was still the head of the Eon team, but as he got older, members of his family were assuming greater responsibility for the films. Cubby co-produced *The Living Daylights* with Michael G Wilson, who also co-wrote the script with Richard Maibaum. Michael had been Dick's writing partner on every script since *For Your Eyes Only*.

I had known Cubby's daughter Barbara since she was a little girl, and she'd been contributing to the films in various capacities for the last ten years. She has a great instinct for casting and this, among her many other talents, was formally recognised with a promotion. On *The Living Daylights* she served as one of the associate producers, alongside Tom Pevsner.

Timothy's 007 is revealed in a tense pre-titles sequence shot in Gibraltar, and this was the first place we visited on our location reconnaissance. The mountainous landscape was the perfect backdrop to some of the most amazing stunt driving to appear in any Bond film.

From Gibraltar it was only a short hop to Spain, where we met Denise O'Dell. Denise is the daughter of the film producer Denis O'Dell, who was best known for his collaborations with The Beatles. Denise is now a producer in her own right, but on *The Living Daylights* she was the production manager of the Spanish shoot.

OPPOSITE PAGE: Kamran Shah's Mujahedin attack a Soviet air base in Afghanistan. This sequence was staged more than 4,000 miles away, at Ouarzazate in Morocco.

ABOVE: Maryam d'Abo (as Kara Milovy), Timothy Dalton (as James Bond) and director John Glen, on location in Vienna.

BELOW: We filmed the pre-titles sequence in Gibraltar.

RIGHT: My sketch of M's office, which is revealed to be aboard a Hercules military transport plane flying over Gibraltar.

FAR RIGHT: M (Robert Brown) struggles to retain the paperwork on his desk as his 00 agents parachute from the open loading ramp.

BELOW LEFT: Joe Don Baker as Brad Whitaker.

BELOW RIGHT: Examples of Whitaker's sophisticated armaments appear from drawers beneath his wargame dioramas.

Denise also arranged our visits to Tangier, where we visited a house owned by Malcolm Forbes, the American entrepreneur who published *Forbes* magazine. It was an amazing place, but we were most impressed by his extensive private museum of miniature soldiers, which provided the inspiration for the collection owned by arms dealer Brad Whitaker (Joe Don Baker) in the film. We recreated Malcolm Forbes' dioramas at Pinewood, including table-top versions of Agincourt, Waterloo and Gettysburg. A company called Little Lead Soldiers provided all the figures, each painted to a beautiful standard. Beneath the tables I designed special drawers that opened to reveal samples of the sophisticated weaponry that Whitaker was trying to sell to General Pushkin (John Rhys-Davies). Much of this set was demolished at the end of the film, when Bond returned for an explosive gun battle with Whitaker.

Our desert location was also in Morocco, near a city called Ouarzazate. This had appeared in numerous previous films, notably *Lawrence of Arabia* (1962), and it would feature prominently in *The Living Daylights*. We flew there in a small private plane, getting the pilot to circle various places that we could reach with no more than an hour's travel by road. In the eastern part of Ouarzazate

province we discovered the Taourirt Kasbah, a fortress made of clay, so we landed nearby and added this to our list of location landmarks.

The local airport gave us permission to shoot pretty much what we wanted, because at that time only one or two flights came in and out of the place every week. We put up sets, applied camouflage and added some military planes to make it look like Afghanistan. There was an army camp nearby, so we asked them to lend us military vehicles, guns and other equipment for added authenticity. The few tourists that did arrive there must have wondered what they'd let themselves in for when they saw all the sandbags and gun emplacements.

My brother Michael loved working with miniatures so he accompanied the visual effects designer John Richardson when he went to Ouarzazate to build an additional runway for our airport. John and Michael's models include the Jeep that Bond and Kara (Maryam d'Abo) use to escape the Hercules and the plane that subsequently crashes into a mountain. John also made the Jeep that flew off the cliff in Gibraltar towards the end of the pre-credits sequence.

TOP LEFT AND RIGHT: Building the runway for the model Hercules sequence at Ouarzazate.

ABOVE: We added a number of sets to make the local airport look like a military base.

LEFT: With my brother, Michael (centre), and one of our Moroccan assistants.

Above left: Filming the attack on the air base set in Ouarzazate.

Above right: When I spotted this relatively low bridge I was convinced it had potential.

Below left and right: Pyrotechnics from the special effects department create the impression the air base is being bombed.

One of John's greatest achievements was the bridge that Bond destroys when he drops a bomb from the cargo bay of the Hercules. I was on a reconnaissance with Barbara, Tom, Michael Wilson and John Glen when we found a gully that was crossed by a low concrete bridge. I remember we were sitting under a palm tree, eating our lunch, when I pointed to this bridge and said that should be the one we used. "That would look ridiculous," said John G. "You can't blow that up – it's only about ten feet off the ground." But I had a feeling that it could be made to work with a bit of help from the special effects department.

When I returned to Pinewood I showed my brother the pictures I'd taken of the bridge. He came up with a cardboard diorama that he asked us to imagine could be placed between the camera lens and the front of the real bridge. This illustrated how a foreground miniature could create the impression that this low concrete structure was actually a tall trestle bridge spanning a large canyon. The model John Richardson built at Pinewood was five feet high. Silicone was used to represent the glistening riverbed and miniature trestles formed the support towers of the bridge. The model was sent out in sections and assembled on location by Michael. After it was placed in position in front of the real bridge, a nodal head was fixed to a tripod, allowing John Glen and his cameraman Alec Mills to move their camera without affecting the perspective of the shot. The results were incredible, and still bear close scrutiny on both the big screen and the high definition broadcasts we see today.

Far left: A foreground miniature made the bridge seem much taller...

Left: ... before we cut to a model shot of its destruction.

Below left: One of the gas lines Tom and I found in Vienna.

Below right: An establishing shot of Vienna from the film.

Bottom right: In this special effects scene the Harrier Jump Jet appears to fly from the top of the gasometer.

Our German and Austrian location manager was Leonhard Gmür. He accompanied Tom and me to Vienna, where the concert sequences would be filmed. It was here that we also found the big gas lines that Bond and Saunders (Thomas Wheatley) would use to smuggle KGB defector General Koskov (Jeroen Krabbé) into Austria. When he comes out of the pipe, the slightly bewildered General is taken to a gasometer before a Harrier Jump Jet parked at the top of the building flies him to safety. The gasometer we used was, I think, a listed building in Vienna. There was nothing inside it except the huge staircase you can see the General climbing in the film. Our stills man, Alan White, took a photograph of the gasometer which we used as the basis of a matte over scenes we shot later at the Harrier base in RAF Wittering. The plane appears to emerge from the top of the gasometer in Vienna, but in fact it never left the UK.

When we finished looking around Vienna, Leonhard showed us a number of mountainous locations. We had originally intended to feature an ice yachting sequence, and Tom and I had looked at some people participating in this precarious sport on a frozen lake near Munich. I was highly disturbed by the cracking noises the ice made beneath my feet, so I don't know how anyone had the courage to send a boat skimming across the top of it. We got hold of an ice yacht back at Pinewood and were thinking about how to adapt it, when it was decided to rewrite the sequence as a car and ski chase. The new location would be a lake south of Vienna, where Bond's Aston Martin V8 would sprout one more gadget in the shape of outriggers that drop from beneath the doors into a fixed position alongside the wheels.

Right: Bond's Aston Martin makes a getaway across a frozen lake.

Far right: Bond steers the car in a circle, cutting a hole in the ice.

Below left: The rocket that propels the car over the bank of the lake.

Below right: A publicity shot of the Aston Martin showing its ice-cutting front wheel and outriggers.

The V8 Vantage Volante that appeared in the film was on loan from Aston Martin. When I originally approached the company for a car the chairman, Victor Gauntlett, offered us his own pre-production model. He even drove it out to Vienna for us, and it's his car you can see in Q's workshop. Victor later sold Cubby a Volante and he was even offered a small role in the film as a KGB colonel. He said he was tempted, but unfortunately running Aston Martin took up too much of his time.

As pre-production continued I had to go back to Aston Martin to buy three more V8s, which Tom and I collected from the company's factory in Newport Pagnell. One was going to have the outriggers fitted and another was going to have all the other devices activated by Bond during the chase. The third would make the rocket-propelled jump over the banks of the frozen lake, blowing up shortly after Bond presses its self-destruct button.

A Lada police car pursuing Bond across the lake meets a less spectacular end when one of the razor-sharp rims of the V8's wheels carves a large hole in the ice. The Lada sinks through the hole into the water underneath. This scene was filmed in the tank at Pinewood and seamlessly cut into the location footage by editors Peter Davies and John Grover.

Following the destruction of the V8, Bond and Kara make their getaway by using Kara's open cello case as a toboggan. Sitting inside the case, they bump down the mountain while Bond uses the spike of Kara's Stradivarius as a makeshift rudder. This sequence was John Glen's idea, and he fought for it during pre-production. Once he'd convinced Cubby it was worth trying I had the job of finding three or four cellos – and cases – that all looked similar, so we'd have spares to take the place of those that would inevitably be damaged. My old friend Bert Davey was one of the additional art directors on the picture and found a cello dealer who said he could help us. Unfortunately this bloke never seemed to be in his shop when we visited. He drove me nuts, but we got there in the end.

I think the action sequences in *The Living Daylights* are some of the best in any Bond film, and Timothy Dalton was a worthy successor to Roger. In the art department we were generally ahead of the filming, and our work was often done before actors even arrived on set. From what I saw of Timothy, however, he certainly took the role seriously, discussing his motivation with John Glen and creating the impression that he was acting the role of James Bond, rather than falling back on his personality to bring the character to life. Timothy was always very nice to me and my colleagues, remembering everyone's names and taking time to find out what everyone on the set was doing. From our point of view the role of James Bond was in safe hands, and we hoped that audiences would feel the same way.

Above left: With Cubby at the British premiere, being presented to the Prince of Wales.

Above right: The French premiere was attended by Rémy Julienne, Maryam d'Abo, Timothy Dalton, Barbara Broccoli, Cubby and Dana, John and Janine Glen, and marketing director Jerry Juroe.

Below: Bond and Kara find a novel use for a cello and its case.

LICENCE TO KILL

Cubby Broccoli had never forgotten the overspend on *Moonraker* back in 1979, and was proud of the fact that we kept tighter control of our budgets during the 1980s. He pointed out to me that, despite inflation and other rising costs within the film industry, we didn't match the budget of *Moonraker* until we made *Licence to Kill*, which was released ten years later.

The financial pressures placed on Cubby by MGM/UA were partly prompted by the performance of the films – box-office admissions had been declining since *Octopussy*, and with *The Living Daylights* there was a concern on the part of the distributor that our new Bond, Timothy Dalton, had yet to be wholly accepted by the American audience. The films were still successful, however, and there was no question of anyone other than Timothy playing Bond in *Licence to Kill*.

Extra scrutiny from MGM/UA meant that we had to find ever more inventive ways to make the money go further. The abolition of certain tax breaks in England and a weak dollar made Pinewood prohibitively expensive. When I made my first reconnaissance for *Licence to Kill* in early 1988 we weren't just looking for locations – we were looking for a new studio.

A strike called by the Writers' Guild of America prevented Richard Maibaum from delivering anything other than an outline for the new film, so the screenplay would be solely credited to Michael G Wilson. This relatively violent, uncompromising story would depict Bond going rogue to avenge a savage attack on his old friend Felix Leiter (David Hedison) and the murder of Felix's bride Della (Priscilla Barnes). Bond's vendetta would see him pursue Franz Sanchez (Robert Davi), the ruthless drug baron responsible.

The working title was *Licence Revoked*, and Michael was still developing his script when he joined associate producers Barbara Broccoli and Tom Pevsner, director John Glen and myself on a trip to Florida. We found a number of locations at Key West, including the Overseas Highway and the church where Felix and Della get married, both of which were featured in the pre-titles sequence. M (Robert Brown) would strip Bond of his 00 status during

Opposite page: Filming at Casa Arabesque. From left to right – gaffer electrician John Tythe (standing), Robert Davi (as Franz Sanchez), Timothy Dalton (as James Bond), director of photography Alec Mills, script supervisor June Randall and director John Glen.

Above left: Members of the crew in Key West. From left to right – John Glen, camera grip 'Chunky' Huse, a local driver, cameraman Mike Frift, June Randall, focus puller Frank Elliott, Alec Mills and clapper loader Simon Mills.

Above right: In Key West with Ken Court, one of my art directors.

ABOVE LEFT: The interior of the Barrelhead Bar was a set we built at Churubusco Studios in Mexico City.

ABOVE RIGHT: The coastguard's helicopter grabs Sanchez' plane in this scene filmed at Key West.

BELOW LEFT AND RIGHT: The prison van is hijacked, in another sequence shot in Florida.

an angry confrontation filmed at Ernest Hemingway's house on Truman Avenue, and elsewhere in Key West the Harbor Lights Bar doubled for the Barrelhead Bar in the Bahamas.

A plane from Perry Oceanographics took us to Lee Stocking Island in the central Bahamas. The research centre on the island was established by John H Perry Jr, the company's founder, and ran on wind power. Mr Perry was dedicated to renewable energy and finding ways to breed fish for Third World countries. Although we didn't film anything on the island, the Perry facility gave me inspiration for the interior of the *Wavekrest*, the research vessel owned by Sanchez' associate Milton Krest (Anthony Zerbe).

Elsewhere in the Bahamas we went to George Town before visiting Martinique and Guadalupe. We didn't find locations in every place we went but it was a useful process, if occasionally alarming. In St Croix, Michael hired a taxi driver for a day to show us around, but we decided we'd seen enough by lunchtime. The driver was paid in full, but was so angry about our decision to leave early that he chased us with his tyre irons!

We'd been all over the Caribbean by the time we returned to Miami, where we then caught a plane to Mexico City. As well as some major locations in the film, we were there to look at a studio recommended by Eon's production accountant Douglas Noakes. Churubusco Studios was built by Howard Hughes in the mid-1940s but was now being run by the Mexican government.

As I walked past one of the caravans on the lot a door opened and Gregory Peck emerged. Greg was one of the kindest and friendliest people I ever met in the film business. In 1974 he had produced a film called *The Dove*, employing me as his art director on a memorable shoot that had taken me around the world. I hadn't seen him since we made *The Boys from Brazil* in 1978 but he recognised me immediately. "What the hell are you doing here?" he exclaimed, and I joked that I was retracing

my steps from *The Dove*, travelling the world the other way round.

Greg was making a film called *Old Gringo*, and the comedy *Honey, I Shrunk the Kids* was also filming at the studio. Once I got inside and had a look around I was amazed that this antiquated facility was able to sustain this level of production. Churubusco was in disarray, and I considered that whatever economies Douggie Noakes had identified wouldn't make it worth coming here.

We flew back to Los Angeles for a meeting with Cubby. "OK Peter," he said, reclining in his leather chair. "What do you think?" I didn't hold back. "It's a big studio," I said, "but it's a dump. The roof leaks, the phones don't work and there are no facilities. It needs a bloody makeover. We should make this one the way we normally do it – shoot the locations out there and then come back to Pinewood for the studio."

Cubby listened to what I said but didn't look up from his desk. "If we don't make the picture in Mexico City then we're not making the picture." So that was that. We would just have to make it work.

We returned to Mexico City after Easter, and I braced myself for the task ahead. Many of the things we took for granted in England weren't available in Mexican shops at that time. As the advance guard of the art department I had to bring pencils, pens and paper – the basic tools of my trade. At Churubusco we installed a telephone system, fax machines and an art department complete with workshops. While we were at it we fixed the roof.

There was some compensation in the fact that during my extended stay in Mexico I was joined by my wife Ann. We shared a house in a street called Corredores with my brother Michael, who was the co-art director, and his wife Yvonne. The construction manager Tony Graysmark and his wife Margaret also stayed with us. The house had been built in the 1940s but its design was medieval. Some of its facilities seemed almost as old – we'd experience power cuts when the landlady failed to pay the electricity bill, and the water would have a habit of drying up when you were halfway through

Top left: Timothy was very thorough in his research for the role of Bond, even styling his hair to match the description Fleming gave in the novels.

Top right: Members of my art department at Churubusco, including assistant art director Andrew Ackland-Snow, assistant art director Richard Holland, assistant Simon Lamont, artist Bob Walker and assistant art director Neil Lamont.

Above: Enjoying the night life in Mexico City with my wife Ann.

RIGHT AND FAR RIGHT: Building the interior sets of the oil refinery at Churubusco.

BELOW LEFT: The interior of Felix Leiter's house.

BELOW RIGHT: The interior of Sanchez' office was a good example of the Mexican crew's craftsmanship.

a shower. You'd have to shout to the maid downstairs, asking her to pump some more to the bathroom. There was no hot water at all until we got a plumber in.

Every morning a minibus driven by a guy called Chu Chu would take Michael, Tony and myself on the ten-minute drive to work. The studio was so near that some days we would cycle there instead. My son, Neil, was also on the picture as one of the assistant art directors and one of his assistants in the art department was my nephew Simon. Supreme nepotism! But, as ever, I made sure that each of them gave 150 per cent.

Tony brought one of his plasterers and one of his decorators to Mexico. The construction crews there all worked in groups of 16, and I was impressed that they watched us so carefully and were so willing to learn. This was a marked contrast to my memories of *Moonraker*, where the crews in France just didn't want to know when we tried to show them how we wanted things done.

Many of the interiors you see in the film were shot on location, but we often had to build matching sets in the studio for close-ups. I was amazed by the craftsmanship that went into Milton Krest's laboratory, while Sanchez' office was built to exactly match location shots of the big theatre – El Teatro de la Ciudad – in Mexico City. The interior of the office was made of mahogany, which was French-polished to a higher standard than I would have expected from a French crew. The Mexicans had power tools at their disposal, but given a choice they did everything by hand – even painting both sides of an office door when only one side would be seen by the camera. I admired their dedication and diligence.

While the boys were building the sets at Churubusco my brother and I flew back to Key West where I met Ned Kopp, who was production supervisor for the Florida shoot. We only had a couple of days to find everything else we needed before Michael G Wilson and John Glen arrived. Their

plane was only 20 minutes away from landing when we finally found the last location – a property in South Street that we used for Felix Leiter's house and patio.

By this time I had been feeling ill for quite a few weeks. It had started on a hiking trip, when I experienced a sticky sensation in my hands and a heaviness in my legs. I put it down to all the flying I'd done and tried to forget about it. As the weeks went on I gained a lot of weight, and Ann said that I started snoring so loudly that the bed was shaking. In Key West I was finally persuaded to see a doctor. I had barely walked through the door when he said, "Son, you don't look too good." He took a blood sample and told me to come back at the end of the week for the results. On Friday I went to the local hospital and met another alarming doctor, who told me my blood was "like oil" and that I was "on the way out". I was suffering from hypothyroidism and needed urgent medication. He gave me a bottle of pills and told me to take two a day, starting immediately. When I woke up the following morning it was like a veil had been lifted. I felt so much better that when my brother suggested we hired a boat and went sport fishing I accepted immediately.

When I went back to work on Monday I discovered that Cubby and his wife Dana had heard about my problems. Cubby's cousin, James D'Orta, was a doctor with the paramedic group Lifestar International. Cubby asked 'Dr Jim' to fly to Mexico City, where he kept an eye on me and the other members of the crew.

Apart from Key West, there were other locations that were as exotic as almost anything we'd built for the previous Bond films. The Olimpatec Meditation Institute in the fictional Republic of Isthmus may look like a base designed for one of the series' more extravagant villains, but it came to us virtually ready-made.

Top: Talisa Soto (as Lupe Lamora), John Glen and Timothy Dalton rehearse a scene at a disused casino in Mexico City.

Above: An outing with Ann, Ken Court (far right) and others.

Far left: Sanchez' plane on the backlot at Churubusco Studios.

Left: With Ann, visiting a street market outside Mexico City.

ABOVE LEFT: Standing in front of the Otomi Ceremonial Center.

ABOVE RIGHT: Some of the cone-like structures John spotted above the trees.

BELOW: Cubby and Dana Broccoli (centre) stayed at Casa Arabesque while we shot there.

The Centro Ceremonial Otomí, or Otomi Ceremonial Center, had only recently been built in an effort to preserve and celebrate the customs and culture of the indigenous Otomi people. This sprawling monument is some 7,000 feet above sea level but was still virtually impossible for us to find when Héctor López, our Mexican production supervisor, told us about it. John Glen and I must have spent three hours driving around Temoaya until John spotted the Center's cone-like structures poking out above the dense forest of pine trees. We couldn't believe our luck when we explored the place, and were just as pleased to be told that it was hardly ever used. With the help of some foreground miniatures created by my brother, the OMI Institute received both trucks and helicopters in its role as the nerve centre of Sanchez' operation.

Another case in point was Sanchez' palatial villa, which was not a purpose-built set but a property called Casa Arabesque overlooking Acapulco Bay. Arabesque was the winter home of Baron Enrico di Portinova, a friend of Cubby and Dana's. The house had been completed in 1982 after six years' construction and I could see why it had taken so long – there were three swimming pools, a helicopter pad, a basement nightclub and even a waterfall, which the Baron had installed for his wife, Cindy. On the roof was a camel train carved in alabaster, while beneath it was a dining room that could seat 60 people. I assumed that the Baron and his guests could eat there whenever they liked, but to my surprise the estate manager told me that anyone wanting a meal had to give two weeks' notice!

Left and far left: The incredible tanker chase through the Rumorosa Pass and its explosive conclusion.

Below left: With Ann and assistant art director Richard Holland.

Below right: In 1988 our neighbour, Peter Hinson, gave me this sketch depicting our adventures in Mexico.

A previously unused section of Ian Fleming's novel *Live and Let Die* was the inspiration for the harrowing sequence where Leiter is maimed by Sanchez' pet shark. This and the other underwater filming was undertaken off the coast of Cancún by Ramón Bravo, a talented cameraman who lived locally.

The other major location was a three-mile stretch of highway in the Rumorosa Pass, outside Mexicali, where John and his second unit director Arthur Wooster spent seven weeks filming the truck chase that formed the climax of the film. Rémy Julienne and his team of drivers excelled themselves and the pyrotechnics, engineered by John Richardson and Chris Corbould, were the most spectacular yet seen in a Bond movie.

Mexico had been a steep learning curve for all of us. Shortly after they arrived I overheard Barbara saying to Michael, "Why the hell have we come here?" But she rose to the challenge and played a large part in ensuring that production ran smoothly. Along the way I gained a deep respect for the hard-working crews – in fact I returned to Mexico on three subsequent occasions to make films.

We received a bonus for finishing the film a week ahead of schedule, and with some time in hand Ann told me she'd like to visit Oaxaca. Neil drove us there, and we all stayed in a beautiful old monastery.

When I saw the edited film some months later I told John Glen that it was a bloody good picture – possibly the best he'd made. We were all disappointed when its release in summer 1989 put it up against *Lethal Weapon 2* and *Batman*, two films that American audiences in particular found more appealing. *Licence to Kill*'s relatively disappointing box-office triggered a period of behind-the-scenes turmoil that would see the departure of John Glen, Richard Maibaum and eventually Timothy Dalton, while a takeover of MGM/UA prompted Cubby to take legal action against the new owner in an effort to defend the shared ownership of Eon's assets.

These problems couldn't really have come at a worse time for Cubby, who was now in his 80s and suffering poor health. He used to say that making movies was what kept him alive, and though he loved working he had to leave Mexico City after a couple of months because the terrible air got to his lungs. He recovered as soon as Dana brought him back to Los Angeles, and I was pleased that he seemed to be back to his old self at the Hollywood premiere of the film in July 1989. I still get emotional when remembering that this was the last time I saw him.

343
343

GOLDENEYE

Although I knew MGM/UA was under new management, it was a while before I became fully aware of the implications for Cubby, Michael and Barbara. While Eon's legal action continued I kept myself busy elsewhere. I received a phone call from Sidney J Furie, who had directed *The Ipcress File* back in 1964. Sid asked me to be the production designer on his film *The Taking of Beverly Hills* (1991) and I brought many members of my team with me, including my son Neil as the art director, set decorator Michael Ford, construction co-ordinator Tony Graysmark and property buyer Ronnie Quelch. Around this time I also made a picture called *Eve of Destruction* (1991) for director Duncan Gibbins.

When Michael and Barbara called me about the next James Bond film, the project had no title and Timothy Dalton was still going to be the star. Along with Tom Pevsner, Douggie Noakes and Iris Rose, I was hired on half pay for three or four months before pre-production was halted amid the ongoing battle with Giancarlo Parretti, the Italian financier who had bought MGM in 1990. I don't remember much about what I did on the version of 'Bond 17' that never got made, except conducting a lot of research into robotics.

The years that followed were lean ones for me. Ann and I had money in the bank and our mortgage wasn't huge, but we enjoyed a comfortable lifestyle and by 1993 our savings were starting to run out. A phone call from Stephanie Austin, saying that her co-producer James Cameron wanted to see me, was very welcome indeed.

In 1988 I'd spent two or three weeks talking to Jim about *The Abyss*, his follow-up to *Aliens*, before my commitments on *Licence to Kill* took me back to England, and then Mexico. Fortunately Jim didn't bear me a grudge, because he asked me to be the production designer of his next movie, *True Lies* (1994). The film starred Arnold Schwarzenegger and cost over $100 million to make. It was by far the biggest production I'd ever been involved

Opposite page: Bond's tank detaches part of a statue on its rampage through St Petersburg – in reality the former runway at Leavesden Studios.

Above left: With my son Neil and brother Michael in the Leavesden art department.

Above right: Pierce Brosnan, the new James Bond, with producer Michael G Wilson, executive producer Tom Pevsner and producer Barbara Broccoli.

BELOW LEFT: The *GoldenEye* art department was in the administration block of a former Rolls-Royce factory in Leavesden.

BELOW RIGHT: Michael Brown helped us to install soundstages in one of the disused factory buildings.

in, and when it was released a number of critics suggested that Jim was using its espionage theme to somehow create a rival to, or even a replacement for, the dormant Bond series. Speaking as someone who was there, I can only say that this was never discussed by anyone on the production team, including Jim. Harry Tasker, the agent Arnold played in the film, had a wife (Jamie Lee Curtis) who was bored out of her mind and the couple had an unruly teenage daughter (Eliza Dushku). This was hardly a situation James Bond would ever find himself in.

I returned home from *True Lies* on a Friday at Easter 1994. The following Monday I reported for duty at Eon, relieved that their legal problems had now reached a positive resolution. Bond 17 would start from scratch, with Michael and Barbara in charge as producers. Things had moved on since I'd last seen them. Timothy Dalton had stepped aside and Pierce Brosnan, an actor who'd come very close to playing Bond in *The Living Daylights*, was now free to take the role. Dick Maibaum had passed away in early 1991, and a young screenwriter called Michael France had submitted a script called *GoldenEye*. Cubby was no longer well enough to play an active role in the day-to-day running of a picture, but kept in touch with Michael and Barbara on a regular basis.

The first challenge for the art department was one I didn't see coming – once again, we had no studio. Pinewood was fully booked with the Sean Connery film *First Knight*, and another movie coming in straight after. Tom Pevsner was promoted to executive producer for *GoldenEye*, and together we went all over England looking for somewhere to base the film. Hatfield Aerodrome, which Steven Spielberg would use for *Saving Private Ryan* (1998), was an early contender, but we eventually settled on a former Rolls-Royce factory at Leavesden in Hertfordshire.

The site was easy to reach, but there were a number of other things that made it appealing. There were two huge buildings which Rolls-Royce had used to make aeroplane engines, and adjoining them was a runway 100 feet wide and 1,500 feet long. Michael Brown, the architect we'd hired for *You Only Live Twice* and both versions of the 007 Stage, helped us to transform this former factory into a fully functioning studio. We didn't use Factory 1 at this point but soundproofed sections of Factory 2 and built five stages inside it. The

former administration building housed the production offices, art department and canteen, while a smaller building around the corner was used for dressing rooms. Even the old control tower was used as a vantage point to film certain special effects sequences.

As the construction crews began converting Leavesden, Michael and Barbara told me they had hired Martin Campbell to direct the picture. I had never met Martin, but I was certainly aware of the strong reputation he had forged on the ITV series *The Professionals* (1980) and the groundbreaking BBC drama *Edge of Darkness* (1985). Michael and Barbara gently reminded me that, according to tradition, the director chose both the cinematographer and the production designer. Shortly after this Martin moved into the office next to mine. One day he called me for a chat. "Sweetie," he began, "what was your last picture?" I told him I'd recently finished working on *True Lies*. "James Cameron is my idol," he smiled, extending his hand. I was in. Martin's a lovely man and we worked well together over the subsequent months. He would arrive at five o'clock every morning, and he made it clear to everyone that his office door was always open.

The Iron Curtain had fallen since the production of *Licence to Kill*, so on *GoldenEye* we were free to conduct our first location reconnaissance in Russia. One of the film's set-pieces is a tank chase through the streets of St Petersburg, where Bond causes mayhem at the controls of a stolen T-54/55. Aside from the fact that nothing like this had ever been attempted before, there were a number of issues facing me and Ian Sharp, the second unit director who would handle the sequence.

Above left: In the art department, with some of the storyboards illustrated by Martin Asbury.

Above right: Construction of the soundstages in Factory 2 nears completion.

Far left above: Director Martin Campbell.

Far left below: Second unit director Ian Sharp.

Above left: Some of my staff at work in the art department.

Above right: Applying a miniature camera to a model of one of the sets. This was a technique I would develop on future films.

Below: A composite of Polaroid photos showing an early stage in the construction of the Russian street at Leavesden.

Pierce Brosnan was only due to be in St Petersburg for one week, which was nowhere near long enough to shoot such a complex sequence. After originally offering permits for filming on certain streets, the Russian authorities started getting cold feet. Shooting could still go ahead, but they'd require a $15 million fee and we'd have to promise to pay their bill for any damage caused by the tank. The fee was ridiculous, and given that I had no idea what was already in need of repair, I expressed the view that we should find another way to do this.

Neil was the supervising art director on *GoldenEye*, and we were together in my office when I reminded him that on *The Taking of Beverly Hills* we had recreated a residential American street in Mexico City. Why couldn't we build a St Petersburg street on the runway at Leavesden? I came up with a plan and art director Andrew Ackland-Snow built a model, which I showed to Martin after he'd viewed the daily rushes the following evening. He could immediately see what I was getting at, and asked me to sell it to Mike and Barbara. The next day, we started talking numbers. They asked how much this was going to cost, and Tony Graysmark estimated a million dollars. United Artists, as our distributor had been renamed, were excited about the sequence and promised to contribute some of this shortfall, but where would the rest of the money come from?

I was at home one Sunday afternoon when I received a phone call from Martin. By now I was getting used to his usual term of endearment. “Sweetie,” he said, “can you pop over to the studio?” When I got there he explained how he'd been juggling the budget and the schedule in an effort to make the tank chase possible. “We were going to take Pierce to St Petersburg,” he reminded me. “How about we don't take the first unit to Russia at all?” I raised my eyebrows as he continued. “We're going to need *some* shots, of course, but we should put the money into the tank chase, because

Far left: Jack Wade (Joe Don Baker) meets Bond (Pierce Brosnan) at St Petersburg Airport. This scene was filmed at Epsom in Surrey.

Left: The street where Jack's car breaks down was another British location – Somerset House in London.

Below left: In this picture I'm busy with a walkie-talkie, seemingly oblivious to the fact that members of my family are playing on the tank behind me!

Below right: The tank, complete with Russian statue, heads down the runway for another take.

that's one of the things that's going to sell the picture. Why don't we send Ian's unit to Russia instead?"

The following day Mike and Barbara agreed. Barbara would accompany Ian Sharp to St Petersburg as the second unit producer and Andrew joined them as my art director. A number of shots of the tank chase would be filmed on location, but most of it would be shot on the runway at Leavesden.

Martin asked me to find British locations that would save the first unit having to go to Russia, so that's exactly what we did – Epsom Downs Racecourse became the exterior of St Petersburg Airport, and the courtyard of Somerset House became the crowded street where Jack Wade (Joe Don Baker) attacked his clapped-out car with a sledgehammer. A church near Paddington Station doubled for the church where Natalya (Izabella Scorupco) was captured.

I turned my attention back to the tank chase, and the challenge of building a convincing Russian street on a runway in Hertfordshire. It would be necessary to hire plasterers and painters, and to give them scaffolding so they could access the sides of our fake buildings. I decided to save time, and money, by getting them to plaster and decorate the fronts of the buildings while the scenery was laid out on the ground. We then used scissor lifts and a crane to lift these flats into position by the sides of our road, before the crew made good the joins between each section.

Right and far right: The tank continues its journey through the backlot set.

Below left: I was very proud of what the crew achieved on the Leavesden backlot.

Below right: The statue on top of the tank heads for a collision course with a bridge.

Another advantage of working this way was that the panels could be taken out or interchanged depending on the course the tank was taking. This elaborate outdoor set took 175 people six weeks and four days to complete. I was proud of them for doing it so well and so quickly – they did a super job.

The second unit filmed their scenes in St Petersburg first. The mayor's wife was watching the proceedings from her apartment when she saw the tank smashing through handrails, balustrades and other items of street furniture. Unaware that these were all props that had been deliberately placed in its path, she immediately got on the phone to her husband. Before they knew it, Ian and his crew were surrounded by armed militia. Tony Waye, who was the associate producer, had to go and see the mayor to sort everything out, but from then on everything they did was carefully monitored.

The footage from St Petersburg was carefully integrated with the material shot on the runway backlot. We didn't send Pierce to Russia at all, and I'd defy anyone to point out where St Petersburg ends and Leavesden begins.

The agility and speed of the tank surprised everyone, including Pierce. In Russia, it was strictly limited to a maximum speed of 30 kilometres per hour, but there was no such restriction on the matching tank we hired for use at Leavesden. It roared down the runway, came up a ramp made of sleepers and smashed through a wall. It must have flown about 75 feet, almost wiping out one of the cameras. Quite impressive, considering it weighed 36 tons.

This was my first experience of working with our new James Bond. If he was

Far left above: The film's establishing shot of MI6 headquarters in London.

Far left below: M (Judi Dench) briefs Bond at MI6. I decided to give her office a contemporary style.

Left and below: Putting the finishing touches to the triple-level control centre at Leavesden.

Below: As usual, I found that making a model of the set could be more useful than just presenting a sketch.

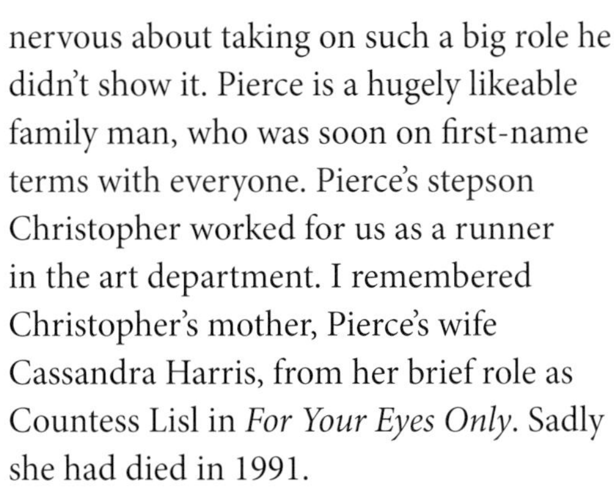

nervous about taking on such a big role he didn't show it. Pierce is a hugely likeable family man, who was soon on first-name terms with everyone. Pierce's stepson Christopher worked for us as a runner in the art department. I remembered Christopher's mother, Pierce's wife Cassandra Harris, from her brief role as Countess Lisl in *For Your Eyes Only*. Sadly she had died in 1991.

The sets we built on the soundstages at Leavesden included the interior of MI6, which underwent a transformation for *GoldenEye*. This was the first film to show the exterior as the distinctive, postmodern landmark at Vauxhall Cross, which became the real headquarters of the British Secret Intelligence Service in 1994. We had a new M, played by Dame Judi Dench, and a new Moneypenny in Samantha Bond. From studying the outside of the Vauxhall Cross building I imagined where their offices might be, and brought the decor up to date. M's office had usually employed traditional, oak-panelled stylings, but for the new place – where she memorably condemns Bond for being a "sexist, misogynist dinosaur" – I went for a more contemporary look. There were still oak wall panels but each one was mounted from floor to ceiling and they were connected by vertical metal trims. These clean lines extended to the furniture, which was modern-looking and functional.

Above: We were delighted when Roger Moore paid us a visit at Leavesden. At one point he joked with Pierce that he'd been asked to take over! This picture shows assistant director Gerry Gavigan, Roger, me and Michael G Wilson.

Below left: This view of the Pilatus Turbo Porter in the pre-titles sequence was filmed in Switzerland.

Below right: Bond and Caroline (Serena Gordon) are pursued by Xenia Onatopp (Famke Janssen) in her Ferrari.

The pre-titles sequence took us back in time nine years, to show Bond and his fellow agent Alec Trevelyan (Sean Bean) breaking into a chemical weapons facility in Soviet Russia. Bond gains access to the roof of the compound by performing a bungee jump from the side of a dam. The 640-feet drop down the Contra Dam, across the River Verzasca in Switzerland, earned the stuntman Wayne Michaels a world record. Soon after, Bond makes his escape from the plant by skydiving from a motorbike into the empty cockpit of a plane that has just plunged off a runway. We used the runway at Leavesden for part of this sequence, building the exterior of the chemical plant on the other side of the Russian street we built for the tank chase. It sounds daft, but it worked.

Although the whole sequence was far-fetched, we wanted to find an aircraft that could plausibly take off from a short runway. I had seen just such a plane – the Pilatus Turbo Porter – in the Mel Gibson film *Air America* (1990). On a visit to the French city of Lyon, Tom and I met someone who owned a Pilatus. We were very impressed by the demonstration he gave us, but our enthusiasm evaporated when we found out how much the planes cost to buy.

Deciding that we didn't always need to feature a working model, I asked a specialist called Mike Woodley to build us an authentic-looking prop from components we sourced separately. After finding a pair of wings from here, a body from there and so on, Mike and the special effects supervisor Chris Corbould assembled a Pilatus at the studio. This elaborate prop was even motor-driven, so its wheels could propel it along the runway.

The scene where the plane and the motorbike launched themselves into the abyss was filmed on top of a mountain near Interlaken in Switzerland. We then cut to a miniature of the plane and close-ups filmed against a green screen in the studio. The only time we ever used a real Pilatus was in the shots of the plane coming out of its dive in Switzerland.

We next see Bond behind the wheel of an Aston Martin DB5, a legendary car indelibly associated with the character. I needed two DB5s for these sequences, which were due to be filmed in France and Monaco, but Aston Martin told me they couldn't help us – after all, they hadn't taken any orders for the car since 1965. They instead directed me to a company outside Norwich that could supply one in red and one in black. When they delivered the cars two weeks later I was delighted to

Far left: Visiting the Russian cruiser *Aurora* on a trip to St Petersburg.

Left: A mock-up of the Tiger helicopter is prepared for filming.

Below left: Filming miniatures of the tank and the armoured train on the backlot at Leavesden.

Below right: The full-size armoured train was based on a diesel locomotive we hired from record producer Pete Waterman.

see that they were both silver, absolutely matching the colour scheme familiar from the DB5's previous appearances in *Goldfinger* and *Thunderball*. I ended up hiring a third silver DB5 from a museum. Rémy Julienne and his drivers once again handled the car stunts, taking great care with the DB5s during Bond's precarious game of cat-and-mouse with Xenia Onatopp (Famke Jansenn). Xenia's Ferrari was not so fortunate, and following a minor accident we had to find another one that matched in order to complete the sequence.

Trevelyan's train depot, and the shots of the full-size exploding train, were filmed at the Nene Valley Railway in Peterborough, where we had previously shot *Octopussy*. The preparations for the armoured train were made at Leavesden, as I figured this would be cheaper than sending a large crew to the Nene Valley for any longer than was necessary. We hired an old Deltic diesel from record producer and train enthusiast Peter Waterman and placed it on some tracks we laid down inside Factory 1. Mike Boone, one of my assistant art directors, did all the drawings that transformed this former British Railways engine into the armoured behemoth you see on screen. We then got hold of some carriages to put on the back. The train was filmed at Nene Valley and the nearby British Sugar factory, where about half a mile of track still survived. The interior was built in the studio.

RIGHT: Derek Meddings' model of the radio telescope at Leavesden.

FAR RIGHT AND BELOW: Shots of the real Arecibo Observatory in Puerto Rico.

The gruelling fight between Bond and Trevelyan took place at the Arecibo Observatory in Puerto Rico. The radio telescope, in operation since 1963, was engaged on something that prevented me from going into the middle of the structure when I made my first reconnaissance there in 1994. We flew in by helicopter, and I remember our pilot was warned to steer well clear of the 18 cables suspending the 900-ton receiver platform above the collecting dish. The dish has a diameter of 1,000 feet, making it the largest of its kind in the world.

This was a stunning location but we completely understood that it would be impossible to switch the telescope off for the extended periods we'd require for filming. The solution was to only show the actual telescope in long shots, while recreating it in miniature in the studio. We took a lot of photographs and measurements which my brother, Michael, used to create plans back in England. The crew I had used on *True Lies* came out to Puerto Rico with us; the country is American territory so they didn't need work permits.

The GoldenEye satellite that is directed from the observatory and the electronic key that activates it were based on designs by Syd Cain, whose history with the Bond movies went all the way back to *Dr No*. He was in his mid-70s when we made *GoldenEye* but still wanted to keep his hand in with storyboarding jobs. He had treated me well when we made *On Her Majesty's Secret Service* and *Live and Let Die*, so I was happy to oblige.

Syd wasn't the only familiar face we welcomed back. Convincing miniatures were crucial to the success of *GoldenEye*, and these were supervised by Derek Meddings, the brilliant special effects designer I had last worked with on *For Your Eyes Only*. Derek was going through a tough time – his marriage had ended and he was having problems with his business, the Magic Camera Company. He wasn't very good with money, and in 1994 he asked me if I could help him to get a job at Eon. He came to our rescue so many times on *GoldenEye*, and the best tribute I can pay to his work on this picture is that you won't actually notice most of it – his miniatures were so beautifully made and filmed that they were indistinguishable from the real thing.

During pre-production Martin Campbell had fallen in love with the idea of shooting the Russian tracking station in Siberia, but it just wasn't practical. We were thinking about going somewhere like Norway or

Far left and left: The destruction of the tracking station and the lake draining above the control centre are a few examples of the sequences Derek created for the film.

Below left: Derek (right) with director of photography Phil Méheux.

Below right: Derek on the model landscape of Siberia he built for *GoldenEye*.

Iceland instead, when an old film gave me an idea. One evening Ann was out so I turned on the television and found myself watching the 1947 classic *Black Narcissus*. The film is set in a convent in the Himalayas but the directors, Michael Powell and Emeric Pressburger, never set foot outside Pinewood Studios, except for some brief scenes shot at a landscaped garden in Sussex. The next day I reminded Derek of this and we decided to fake a Siberian location with some old-fashioned camera tricks. Scenic artist Brian Bishop painted a photographic-quality backing of some mountains, while my brother took a cast from a lump of coal in order to create a foreground landscape of craggy rocks. Into this snowbound setting Derek added models of a Tiger helicopter, the tracking station and the MiG fighter than causes its ultimate destruction. These were just some of the models he made for *GoldenEye*, a film that benefited hugely from his talents.

Derek was ill several times towards the end of the shoot in 1995, and his condition was eventually diagnosed as cancer. On Saturday 9 September I was taking Ann to an appointment at the Nuffield Hospital in Wexham when I discovered that Derek was a patient in one of the wards upstairs. He looked better than I was expecting, but was clearly in low spirits. "Pete," he said, "I don't know what I'm going to do. I'll never be able to work again..." I did my best to reassure him. "Derek, you can *always* come and work for me. You can come to the office and draw or do whatever you want to do." He shook his head, as if he was embarrassed by my offer, but I told him to think about it. "Come on Derek," I said. "How long have we known each other? Remember – we're friends." And with that I left him to get some sleep.

On Monday morning my brother called to tell me that Derek had suffered a heart attack the previous day and died. I knew he was ill but I honestly thought he was going to pull through. My hand was shaking as I solemnly replaced the receiver.

Derek was a lovely man and one of the greatest technicians I ever met. He didn't live to see the release of *GoldenEye*, but I know he would have been pleased that its success gave the James Bond series a new lease of life. The film is dedicated to his memory.

THE WORLD IS NOT ENOUGH

I celebrated my 65th birthday in November 1994, while I was location scouting for *GoldenEye* in Puerto Rico. Michael Ford, my set decorator, made me a bus pass to remind me that I'd now reached retirement age, and that evening I was delighted to receive a phone call from Cubby. It was the first time we'd spoken for several years, and we chatted for a while about how the new film was shaping up. Everyone knew that Cubby hadn't been well, and he told me he was about to go into hospital to have his aortic valve replaced. This was major cardiac surgery, and I wished him well.

The next James Bond film, *Tomorrow Never Dies* (1997), was the first of the Eon films I'd missed since *From Russia With Love*. While I was disappointed not to take part, I joked at the time that I wasn't the sort of guy to desert a sinking ship – I was unavailable because I was the production designer on James Cameron's *Titanic* (1997).

I was working with Jim in 1996 when word reached me that Cubby's condition was now serious. I asked John Parkinson, one of the executives at Eon, if I could go and see Cubby at his home in Beverly Hills. If the time had come to say goodbye, I wanted to do it in person. John spoke to Dana, Cubby's wife, and then called me back. Dana's message thanked me, but said it was probably better not to come. She said it would be better for me to remember Cubby the way he was.

I was heartbroken when Cubby passed away on 27 June. I never met anyone like him. His respect for his crews was legendary, and I had first-hand experience of this kindness. He was always the first at the bar to buy his "boys" a drink at the end of a day's shooting. At his memorial service I consoled myself with the knowledge that he had lived long enough to see the Bond films relaunched, and that he knew his legacy was in safe hands with Michael and Barbara.

Although I wasn't working on *Tomorrow Never Dies*, Michael and Barbara invited me for lunch at their new studio, which was specially adapted from a former warehouse in Frogmore, St Albans. I met the director, Roger Spottiswoode, and the production designer, Allan Cameron. As a general rule I don't go on other people's sets – who would want another production

OPPOSITE PAGE: The model of the MI6 building in Vauxhall Cross is prepped for shooting.

ABOVE: The cast and crew of *The World is Not Enough* on the backlot at Pinewood.

Above left: Director Michael Apted in front of the Guggenheim Museum in Bilbao, where part of the pre-titles sequence was filmed.

Above right: Concept art showing the exterior of the MI6 building after the explosion.

Below: A sketch of the MI6 entrance hall by concept illustrator Robert Cowper.

designer inspecting their work? – but on this occasion I made an exception and I thought Allan did an excellent job.

Titanic was by far the most successful film I ever worked on, and in 1998 I received an Academy Award for Best Art Direction, which I shared with Michael Ford. Mike Wilson and Barbara Broccoli were among the first to congratulate me, sending me a note which began, "Dear Pete, We knew you'd get one eventually." Soon after this Michael Apted, the director of Bond 19, offered me a job on the new film, and of course I accepted.

Michael had earned just as much acclaim for his television documentaries as his feature films, and I thought he was an intriguing choice to direct *The World is Not Enough*. What first impressed me, however, was the assurance from his assistant that "Michael is *never* late." Like Martin Campbell before him, Michael was always early for everything. That's the way I run my life too, so I had a feeling we were going to get on.

The pre-titles sequence began in Bilbao, before moving to MI6 headquarters in London. Since *GoldenEye* I had actually spent some time inside the real building in Vauxhall, but I didn't allow the experience to have any significant influence on my designs for the interiors. I'm committed to authenticity wherever possible, but in this instance I was mindful of security concerns and the demands of the story had to come first.

The World is Not Enough was the first Bond film since *The Living Daylights* to entirely base its studio production at Pinewood. The MI6 sets were built on E Stage, and this is where filming began in January 1999. A stash of exploding bank notes blows a hole in the side of the building, and Bond goes after the mysterious Cigar Girl (Maria Grazia Cucinotta) – the terrorist he suspects is responsible. The longest pre-titles sequence

Far left: With Michael G Wilson, outside the Millennium Dome.

Left: Michael Apted leads the scouting party to the Dome. The building was still under construction when we featured it at the end of the lengthy pre-titles sequence.

Below left: Sketches of the Q Boat by concept illustrator Dominic Lavery.

Below right: Second unit director Vic Armstrong.

in the series' history continues as he pursues her down the Thames and through the streets of London in a jet-powered boat he steals from Q's laboratory.

The Cigar Girl's boat came from a company called Sunseeker in Poole, and the Q Boat was supplied by Bentz. The stunt co-ordinator Simon Crane had suggested using a Bentz boat after seeing some of them competing in a television programme. One of the boats was reserved for use in the studio, while outside the special effects supervisor Chris Corbould adapted a number of others to include an onboard computer, a jet exhaust and heat-seeking missiles. One of them was even capable of briefly diving underwater, and Pierce had so much fun at the controls he didn't mind getting wet. The sequence took certain liberties with the actual geography of the Thames before finishing above the soon-to-be-opened Millennium Dome at Greenwich Peninsula. The building was the subject of some controversy in 1999 and 2000, but I thought the design was amazing. The people that built it did a fantastic job and were very courteous to us.

Like any efficient director, Michael Apted had planned 'weather cover', just in case the conditions in London wouldn't be good enough to shoot on the Thames every day. The weather was fine, however, and things were progressing well when he asked me if the sets at Pinewood were ready. I always got things prepared well in advance, so I told him everything at the studio was ready to go. "Good," he said, before explaining how he proposed to divide the work with the second unit director, Vic Armstrong. "How about I leave Vic to direct the boat sequence during the week, while I work with the first unit at the studio? Pierce and I can then join Vic to shoot our bits with the boat at the weekends." I could see the logic – Vic had his own people on location and could get what he needed without Michael looking over his shoulder.

Above left and right: Two of the sets we built for MI6's remote operations centre in Scotland. The portrait of Bernard Lee's M can be seen on the left.

Below left: The establishing shot of Thane Castle that appears in the film.

Below right: Charles Robinson (Colin Salmon), Bill Tanner (Michael Kitchen) and M (Judi Dench) brief the agents inside the castle.

The attack on the Vauxhall Cross building forces M (Judi Dench) and her staff to relocate to MI6's remote operations centre at Thane Castle in Scotland. The location was Eilean Donan Castle in the western Highlands, but the interiors were entirely built at Pinewood. As with Vauxhall Cross, the interiors didn't match the location, but this was another instance where that didn't bother me at all. For one thing, the castle rooms that I designed for C Stage were far too big to have fitted in the real castle.

Even though this was an emergency bolthole for MI6 I wanted to maintain the air of understated luxury associated with the secret service in the Bond films. I'd recently used oak for the dining room and staircase on *Titanic*, and I decided to do the same thing for the baronial briefing room in the castle. It didn't actually cost that much more than using wood-patterned wallpaper, and was probably cheaper to put up. In a subtle nod to the past, we hung a portrait of Bernard Lee's M behind one of the desks.

The plot of the film revolved around oil pipelines in the Caspian Sea. The setting had been suggested by Barbara after she saw a television documentary, and photographs of the pipes and walkways certainly looked cinematic. On the first reconnaissance I joined Michael Wilson, Michael Apted, line producer Tony Waye and director of photography Adrian Biddle on a trip to Azerbaijan. In Baku, the capital city, we boarded a rickety helicopter for a tour of offshore oil fields. Our ear defenders protected us from the terrible noise of this old helicopter, but I was unprepared for the stench of gas and petroleum.

We continued our tour of the Bibi-Heybat oil field by car, and I was struck by the shambolic state of the equipment – much of it seemed to be falling to bits, and in places they were even using old-fashioned 'nodding donkey' pumpjacks.

Our next trip was to Turkey, where a whistle-stop tour of the country took in parts of the coast, dockyards, the mountainous region of Cappadocia and ultimately Istanbul. The villa owned by Elektra King (Sophie Marceau) was set in Baku, but the exterior was actually filmed here. The exterior of Elektra's Turkish headquarters was also filmed in Istanbul, at a building called Maiden's Tower which sits on a small island in the Bosphorus. This stretch of water separates Europe from Asia, and we crossed from one side to the other, changing from a large boat to a small one along the way. I somehow lost my footing during this changeover and was left dangling on the side of one of these boats, praying I wouldn't fall into the water. Fortunately the quick-thinking Vic Armstrong hauled me back onto the deck.

A happier memory of this trip was an evening I spent in a local restaurant with my son, Neil, who was the supervising art director. Neil's wife, Sarah, had just given birth to their son William, so we all celebrated.

When we came back to England we were presented with a number of problems. Vic had been shooting the ski chase at Chamonix in France when a major avalanche made it impossible to continue. Meanwhile, an assassination in Istanbul had made our insurance company nervous about sending Pierce to Turkey. Michael Wilson asked me to meet him in Barcelona, and from there we found a number of locations in Spain that doubled for the places we had intended to use in Turkey. In the finished film, Elektra's oil pipeline would be established with shots of Azerbaijan, before cutting to scenes filmed in Spain, Wales, Black Park in Buckinghamshire and even model shots created by my brother, Michael, and John Richardson.

ABOVE: A sketch of Elektra's mobile office by Robert Cowper. Much of what Rob illustrated here was cut from the finished film.

LEFT: A Dominic Lavery sketch showing one of the Parahawks that attack Bond and Elektra in the Caucasus Mountains.

BELOW LEFT AND RIGHT: Two views of the location near Zaragoza that we used for the exterior of the Russian nuclear testing facility.

Filming of *The World is Not Enough* dominated Pinewood in the first half of 1999. The interior of the Russian nuclear testing facility was built on the 007 Stage and was my idea of what a silo like this would look like. Following a confrontation with Renard (Robert Carlyle) Bond is left to die against this backdrop of decommissioned nuclear weapons. The exterior of the facility was filmed in Spain, at a site north of Zaragoza that looked like a smaller version of Monument Valley. In 2000 director Terry Gilliam would use the same place to shoot *The Man Who Killed Don Quixote*. A flash flood literally washed away his set, and the film was abandoned. He's made numerous attempts to revive the project ever since and, as of 2016, he's still trying.

The submarine surfaced on Pinewood's E Stage, while its interiors were a particularly complicated set that we constructed on D Stage. The underwater shots of John's model submarines were filmed in the familiar territory of the Bahamas.

The caviar factory owned by Valentin Zukovsky (Robbie Coltrane) was an outdoor set constructed around the paddock tank. Space is money, and at that time Pinewood was getting rid of its stock flats, some of which were up to 30 feet high. We bought a load, which I had painted black and fixed around the edges of the caviar factory. We then got a tower crane to build the walkways that criss-crossed the set.

Bond arrives at the factory in his BMW Z8, a nippy roadster introduced by the

Above left and right: On the set of the submarine interior.

Right: Zukovsky's caviar factory was built around the paddock tank at Pinewood.

Far right: Concept art showing the King helicopters' cutting-edge technology.

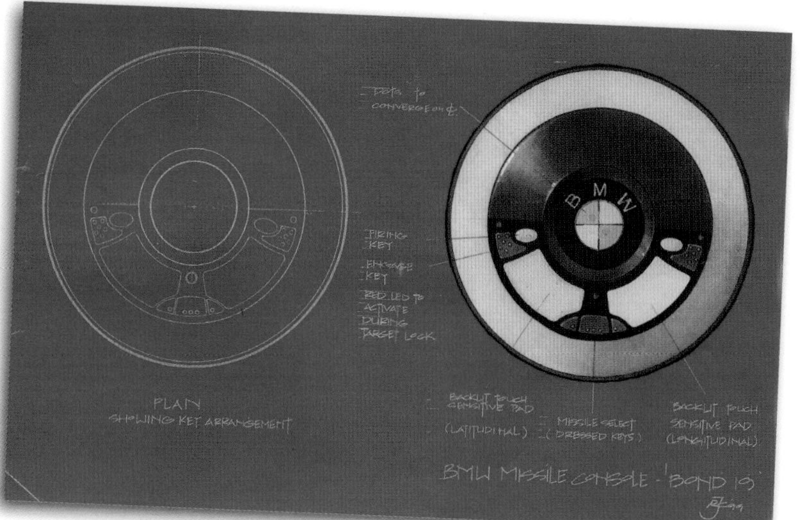

Far left: The Z8 that got destroyed by the helicopter was a copy based on a body supplied by BMW.

Left: Concept art of the missile guidance system built into the car's steering wheel.

Below: Bond (Pierce Brosnan) is tied to Elektra's antique garrotte.

company in 1999. BMW flew us from Luton to their plant in Munich to show us 14 prototypes of the car, but when we explained what we'd need to do to them the colour drained from their faces. Tom Pevsner had retired by this time, but Barbara knew that German was his first language so she asked him to liaise on our behalf. We eventually secured a working car and a body, which Chris Corbould copied at Pinewood. It was one of these props that was destroyed by a King helicopter brandishing a formidable chain of circular saws. "Q's not going to like this..." observes Bond, as the blades tear the car clean in half.

These deadly helicopters might look like something dreamt up for a storyboard, but they were based on real machines. Michael Wilson had wanted to include these suspended saw-blades in a script ever since aerial stuntman BJ Worth had shown him footage of helicopters trimming the tops of tall trees during the making of *Moonraker* in the late 1970s. We had tried to introduce the idea in *GoldenEye*, but it only came to fruition in *The World is Not Enough*, thanks in large part to the tenacity of Chris Corbould.

A less frenzied but equally tense sequence occurred later in the film when Elektra, having shown her true colours, straps Bond to an antique garrotte. As she tightens the wheel at the back of the device she subjects him to an agonising torture that threatens to break his neck.

The ordeal was present throughout the numerous drafts of the script I received, so I had plenty of time to consider my design for the garrotte. My ultimate plans were based on a machine that I'd read about but never seen. I thought it would be interesting to lend an attractive touch to such a brutal device, so I approached a London company called Crisp & Sons who specialised in veneer and other decorative fixtures for furniture. They supplied ornamental strips of wood which we added to the chair ourselves.

I think Ian Fleming would have been pleased that we'd restored the sadistic and slightly kinky element common to so many of his books. In terms of production design, the sequence was also a reminder that amidst the spectacular set-pieces, the Bond films are equally renowned for their attention to fine detail.

DIE ANOTHER DAY

Of all my experiences on the Bond films, I particularly cherish my memories of location scouting with the producers and other crew members who became such good friends.

If you've come this far, you've probably gathered that these trips take place for a number of reasons. They're principally undertaken to identify locations suggested by the script. Sometimes we'd spend time in places that we would decide not to use, and sometimes we'd visit places that we had no intention of using, but these trips weren't wasted, because they'd often provide valuable inspiration for a point of storytelling or for a set I would later design in the studio. Sometimes half a day could be spent in a place that the first unit would occupy for weeks, and sometimes we would spend days in a place that only fleetingly appeared on screen.

All these scenarios, and more, applied to Bond 20, which reached the screen as *Die Another Day* in 2002, the series' 40th anniversary year. Pierce Brosnan's fourth and final outing as 007 was edgy when it needed to be, but elsewhere restored some of the effervescence and outlandish gadgetry I remembered from the Roger Moore blockbusters of the late 1970s.

The high spirits began with the first location reconnaissance. I joined Michael, Barbara, director Lee Tamahori, executive producer Tony Waye and my nephew Simon, who was the supervising art director, on a trip to Newquay in Cornwall. Over the last 25 years, Michael, Barbara and myself had stayed in some unusual places, but we'd never been anywhere like the *Fawlty Towers*-style hotel we endured on this trip.

We were initially glad we'd found *anywhere* to stay, when the booking we'd made at a hotel in St Austell fell through.

OPPOSITE PAGE: A dusting of fake snow is added to the model of the ice palace.

ABOVE LEFT: Concept art of Graves' descent towards Buckingham Palace.

ABOVE RIGHT: With members of the art department on the set of Graves' club. Back row: Paul J Hayes, Ty Teiger, Simon Lamont and James Hambidge. Front row: Katie Gabriel, me and Simon Wakefield.

RIGHT: The beach at Holywell Bay stood in for North Korea.

FAR RIGHT: Bond steals a hovercraft in an attempt to escape from Colonel Moon's North Korean compound.

BELOW LEFT AND RIGHT: Bond surfs into North Korea and arrives on a beach in these concept illustrations by Dominic Lavery.

Our relief turned to bemusement, however, when we met the proprietor of our new place. He didn't just dress like Basil Fawlty – he acted like him too.

After checking in and finding our rooms, we all met downstairs. 'Basil' proceeded to tell us that dinner was already over, but that he had booked us into a local Italian restaurant. On arrival, Michael said, "Let's have some Martinis," but when he placed the order with the waitress she looked slightly puzzled. "Oh..." she said, "I think we've got some of that!" before disappearing behind the bar. Time passed and nothing arrived. After a while Michael said, "I think we've got a problem here," and went off to find her. When he got to the bar he found the staff locked into an argument over our order. Ever the diplomat, Michael said he'd buy a bottle of Martini and make the drinks himself. He requested some ice, before asking, "Do you have a cocktail shaker?" Another puzzled expression, before the girl disappeared again, returning with a couple of pint glasses.

While we were waiting for the food, Tony ordered a couple of bottles of Chianti for our table. We had to settle for one, because that was all they had. We returned to the hotel and were greeted by Basil, who asked us what we'd like to drink. We discovered that one thing the hotel *did* have in abundance was Shrub, an alcoholic cordial popular in Cornwall. So we all ordered a few Shrubs and retired for the evening, slightly worse for wear.

Breakfast was the responsibility of Basil's wife. Let's call her Sybil. Naturally I was expecting the worst, but Barbara seemed very happy with the service. "Wherever

we go, I can never find a soft-boiled egg or toast that isn't overdone," she said. "This," she continued, gesturing with her spoon, "is absolutely perfect." She was so pleased that she even congratulated Sybil. As far as Barbara was concerned, everything was forgiven. I don't think the rest of us were quite so sure.

We were at Newquay in Cornwall looking for a stretch of shoreline for the beginning of the film, when Bond embarks on his ill-fated mission at Pukch'ŏng in North Korea. At the beginning of the process I suggested we should look at Holywell Bay, where I'd been with *Top Secret!* in 1984. We ended up looking at three other beaches, before deciding that Holywell was the place we should have been all along.

Bond is in North Korea to sabotage an arms deal at a military compound run by the corrupt Colonel Tan-Sun Moon (Will Yun Lee). Our original plan was to build the compound at a place overlooking Farnborough Airport, but an objection from the Civil Aviation Authority placed too many restrictions on what we could do with the set. Simon suggested that we should instead build the compound on the Pinewood backlot. He also came up with the idea for the camp's concrete gateway, with its cutting piece that raised and lowered to let trucks and other vehicles in and out.

When Bond's cover is blown he escapes in one of the hovercraft that Moon's soldiers use to glide over the American minefields. The ensuing chase was filmed at the Eelmoor Driver Training Area in Aldershot. Hovercraft are notoriously difficult to steer because they're controlled by air, but the expert drivers on that sequence made sure they looked great on screen.

Above left and right: Dominic Lavery sketches of the hovercraft at Moon's compound.

Below: Dominic's illustration of the compound's cutting piece gateway.

Above left: Working on a model of one of the film's sets.

Above right: With the art department crew outside J Block at Pinewood.

Below left: Bond (Pierce Brosnan) is analysed by a robotic device – in reality a Da Vinci Surgical System.

Below right: We weren't able to film in Havana, Cuba's capital city, but Cadiz in Spain made a highly convincing double.

Bond is captured and tortured by Moon's vengeful father (Kenneth Tsang) for over a year before he's handed back as part of a trade with North Korean terrorist Zao (Rick Yune). We used Ministry of Defence ground for this sequence, and their people built us the Bailey bridge Bond crosses on his short journey from East to West.

During Bond's spell in intensive care he's analysed by a robotic device that feeds data back to some unseen doctors. (We hear one of them say, "Liver not too good," before another replies, "It's definitely him then.") The two-pronged machine hovering over Bond's battered body was a Da Vinci Surgical System, a robotic device capable of performing high-precision operations controlled by a surgeon seated at a connecting console. These machines are in frequent use by the National Health Service, but Michael and Barbara arranged to borrow one from St Mary's Hospital in Paddington in exchange for a donation of £20,000. I visited the hospital and they allowed me to operate the machine for a while, so I could get an idea of how we could use it in the film. Intuitive Surgical, the American company that manufactures

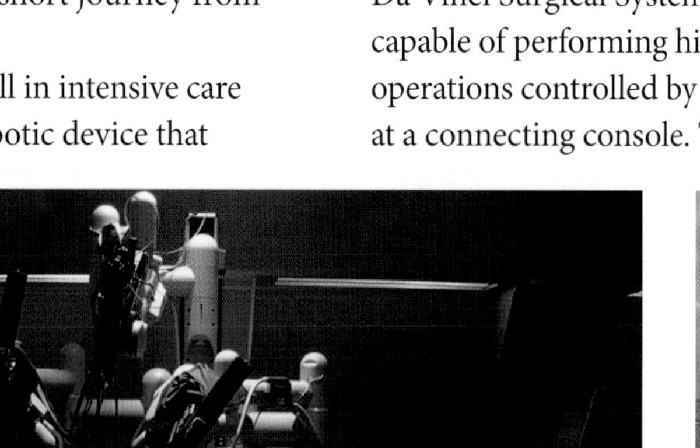

the Da Vinci, heard about this and got in touch to say it would be better if we didn't borrow the hospital's machine. They offered to supply one instead and even sent a technician along to show us how it worked.

One of the film's major settings is Havana, the capital of Cuba, where Jinx (Halle Berry) emerges from the sea in a scene that was designed to pay homage to Ursula Andress' debut in *Dr No*. "Magnificent view," says Bond admiringly, before offering Jinx a Mojito, the local speciality.

Despite the prevalence of Cuba in the film, the US embargo against this communist-ruled country prevented Eon from filming there. We did, however, conduct an extensive reconnaissance in Havana to ensure we could evoke the bustling streets, tobacco factory and other settings as accurately as possible. We had a wonderful time in this vibrant country, with excellent food and live music wherever we went. I even had my first Mojito.

For the purposes of filming we recreated Havana in Cadiz, Spain, with the help of some careful set dressing, a bunch of post-war American cars and a Cuban-flavoured score from the composer, David Arnold.

When the film came out my agent passed on a message from someone who wanted some advice about filming in Cuba. When I called her she asked me how we'd found the country. "We didn't actually film there," I admitted. "We only went to look around. We filmed it in Spain." She refused to believe me, which I suppose I should take as a compliment!

Below left: At La Bodeguita del Medio in Havana. From left to right – director Lee Tamahori, executive producer Tony Waye, producer Michael G Wilson, producer Barbara Broccoli, Michael's wife Jane and me.

Below right: The lovely Halle Berry as 'Jinx' Johnson. I was on the set with Halle one day when I was lucky enough to receive an impromptu kiss. Some of the other crew members were jealous, but I insisted we were just good friends.

ABOVE LEFT AND BELOW: Sketches of the ice palace by Stephen Scott, one of my art directors. Stephen also supervised the building of the interior set.

ABOVE RIGHT: The exterior of the ice palace as it appears in the film.

Five years earlier James Cameron had taken what he called a lipstick camera – so-called because it resembled lipstick on the end of a cable – around the *Titanic* models. Everyone in the camera and art departments could follow this journey by looking at the images on a monitor.

By the time we made *Die Another Day* the technology was even better, and I remember Lee moving a miniature camera around a big model of the ice palace while everyone crowded around to watch. This was the best possible way for me to show my team what I wanted to do, and for Lee to indicate where he wanted the cameras to go. Enthused by the possibilities, Lee asked me, "Suppose I wanted to take cars up the ramp and down the stairs in the ice palace – could we do that?" I said, "Of course. Just let me make sure there's enough steel

The film's most talked-about set was the monumental ice palace built by the villain, Gustav Graves (Toby Stephens), to host a demonstration of his Icarus satellite. As the narrative entered increasingly audacious territory I indulged myself with a design that evoked the ostentatious style of the early Bond films.

My chief inspiration was the work of Santiago Calatrava, a Spanish neofuturist architect whose bridges and buildings are characterised by the kind of curves I incorporated in the spider-like columns that flanked the entrance to the palace. Stephen Scott, one of my art directors, drew most of it up and designed much of the interior. As usual, I decided to demonstrate my intentions with a model.

work in there to support it!" Mike Wilson thought this was a great idea too, so we redesigned parts of the set to accommodate it. Action unit director Vic Armstrong choreographed it beautifully; Zao and Bond skidded their cars around the rapidly melting palace as thousands of gallons of water rained down on them.

The exterior of the ice palace was built on the backlot at Pinewood, although we only created the lower third of the structure. The building was supposed to be 100 feet high, so the rest of it was added as model shots and digital mattes. A company called Snow Business came over and sprayed the ground to make it look naturally frozen. Pierce never went anywhere near real ice or snow, although I hope you wouldn't realise that from watching the film.

The interior of the palace was partly inspired by Icehotel, an incredible establishment constructed every winter in Jukkasjärvi, Sweden, using ice from the River Torne. Our huge set was built on several levels inside the 007 Stage. The walls, doors and ceilings were mostly fashioned from sheets of hard, transparent plastic that were drizzled with wax and sprayed with glitter. All the ice furniture was specially made out of moulded plastic, including the magnificent swan bed in Bond's room. I knew it would be an eye-catching addition to the set, but I didn't dare tell Barbara how much it had cost.

The floor of the palace was supposed to be made of ice as well, and I wanted this to be slick and pure white. Of course, when water freezes over the ground it actually appears to be black, but I knew this wouldn't look right on screen. So I had the floor sprayed white and rubbed down until there were no imperfections. It looked beautiful. We dressed the set, and then Lee decided it would be a good idea to add mist, to help create the impression the building was a giant freezer. This Cardice had a terrible effect on the finely polished floor, which soon ended up looking like a scuffed skating rink. We had to cover it with a layer of sand and spray it all over again. It was never quite the same.

Top left: Members of the art department on the ice palace interior set.

Top centre: The original floor of the set was smooth and white before it was damaged by Cardice.

Top right: On the backlot with the full-size elements that were built for the exterior.

Above left: Miranda Frost (Rosamund Pike) and Bond (Pierce Brosnan) by the swan bed that took a big chunk of my budget.

Left: Inspecting the set during construction at Pinewood.

RIGHT: A Dominic Lavery illustration of the domes above Gustav Graves' diamond mine.

BELOW: Location scouting in Iceland.

BOTTOM: The frozen lagoon where we filmed the car chase.

The setting for the ice palace, and Graves' neighbouring diamond mine, was Iceland. We'd been to Iceland before, for the pre-titles sequence in *A View to a Kill*, but this time we needed to shoot a much more ambitious chase, pitting Zao's Jaguar XKR against Bond's Aston Martin Vanquish.

We originally considered filming in Alaska, and I joined Vic and a number of other guys from the crew on a trip to the Spencer Glacier. When we arrived I was given ski boots and thick snow gear, before I climbed on the back of Vic's snowmobile. I clung on for dear life as he roared off into the snow, but when he pulled a sharp turn I went flying off in the other direction!

Days after this trip we got news that the glacial lagoon at Jökulsárlón in Iceland – where we'd filmed *A View to a Kill* – was now sufficiently frozen to support the weight of several cars, so this was where we headed next. Along with Lee, Michael, Simon and Tony I flew into Höfn, near the Hornafjörður fjord, aboard a private plane. After an overnight stay in a hotel we went to the lagoon, which is at the base of a huge glacier. The shape, durability and colour of the terrain changes enormously throughout the year – for much of the time the icebergs are a dirty white, but when winter sets in they turn a translucent blue. As we gazed across this frozen lagoon there was no doubt in our minds that this should be the setting for the ice palace and the actual location for the car chase.

Vic's unit arrived at the lagoon to shoot the chase in March 2002. They were initially hampered by sub-zero temperatures that made filming – and the operation of the cars – virtually impossible, but they eventually got what they needed before the temperature rose and the ice began to thaw. Stunts where the cars had to flip over and crash into the ground were far too dangerous to film at the lagoon, even when the ice was at its thickest, so the sequence was completed in the more manageable surroundings of a former Ministry of Defence base outside Oxford. There was a clear horizon to the west of this base, so we filled it with photographic cut-outs of icebergs and a number of three-dimensional icebergs that could be wheeled into position. It sounds ridiculous, but once everything was covered with fake snow it was a seamless addition to the location footage.

The supposedly eco-friendly mining operation next to the ice palace was another setting that was never actually built in Iceland. Inspired by Cornwall's Eden Project – a complex of vast greenhouses containing thousands of tropical plant species – the lush interior of our dome was constructed on E Stage at Pinewood. We only included shots of the real Eden Project when we needed to show the ceiling of one of its domes.

When Bond swims under the ice to gain entry to the mine he clasps a pen-like device between his teeth so he can breathe beneath the water. This was one of several nods to *Thunderball* in a script that included references to all of the Eon Bond films that had preceded it. Surveying all the vintage props we gathered in Q's cluttered workshop was like seeing my life flash before my eyes – so many reminders of a film series that had dominated nearly 40 years of my working life.

For some time Ann, my wife, had been trying to persuade me to retire, but my work gave me so much satisfaction that I didn't even want to think about doing anything else. I'd just turned 73 when *Die Another Day* was released, but I felt I had at least one more film in me. Perhaps appropriately, this would be the film that brought us back to the very beginning of the James Bond story.

LEFT: Bond annoys Q (John Cleese) by fiddling with the jet pack from *Thunderball*.

BELOW LEFT: Dominic Lavery concept art for an early design of Zao's Jaguar.

BELOW RIGHT: Madonna played Verity, the fencing mistress, and signed this picture for me when I met her at Pinewood.

TB-6

CASINO ROYALE

Casino Royale was the Ian Fleming book than began it all. First published in 1953, the novel was a heady cocktail of glamour, easy living and sadistic violence that had a profound impact on post-war popular fiction. In 1962 the James Bond phenomenon had a similarly transformative effect on cinema with the release of *Dr No* and... well, you know the rest.

Casino Royale occupies a seminal place in the Bond canon, but an adaptation of the book had always been conspicuous by its absence from Eon's list of official films. The rights to the novel lay elsewhere, and the only big screen version was a self-indulgent comedy starring Peter Sellers. I'd always considered that the existence of the 1967 film precluded Eon from making a more legitimate version of the story, but from talking to Michael Wilson and Barbara Broccoli I discovered that Harry Saltzman and especially Cubby had never given up hope.

The rights to film *Casino Royale* finally came to Eon via a circuitous legal route, and pre-production began in late 2003. This would be one of the most faithful Fleming adaptations in the entire series, and as such would depict Bond's first mission as part of the 00 division. Pierce had been popular with audiences and we were all sad to see him go, but starting fresh dictated the casting of a younger leading man.

It seems hard to believe now, but a degree of cynicism surrounded the casting of Daniel Craig when the announcement was made in 2005. I can say with all honesty that I thought he was an inspired choice, clearly better suited to the role than some of the other contenders. Bond has already attained the rank of commander in the Royal Navy when we're introduced to the character, so hiring an actor in his early 20s wouldn't have made any sense at all. Daniel was in his mid-30s when Michael and Barbara chose him to play Bond, and I reckon that's the perfect age.

OPPOSITE PAGE: Daniel Craig (as James Bond) on the casino set at Barrandov Studios in Prague.

ABOVE LEFT: A 1963 edition of Ian Fleming's novel, with a cover designed by Raymond Hawkey.

ABOVE RIGHT: Producer Barbara Broccoli, Daniel Craig, director Martin Campbell and producer Michael G Wilson in October 2005.

ABOVE: Bond earns his licence to kill in the violent pre-titles sequence.

BELOW LEFT: The establishing shot of the building where Bond assassinates the traitorous Dryden in the pre-titles sequence. The location was a new office block in Prague.

BELOW RIGHT: The exterior of the Hotel Splendide was the Grandhotel Pupp in Karlovy Vary.

When we started filming *Casino Royale* in January 2006 I was sympathetic to Daniel because of the negative press he had unfairly received, but also because he was coming in cold to a situation where everybody else already knew each other. Michael and Barbara were joined by Eon veterans Tony Waye and Callum McDougall as executive producers, and in the art department I recruited my brother Michael and nephew Simon. A number of my other colleagues from the old days had either retired or in some cases passed away, but it was good to welcome back Bernie Hearn, the standby props man I'd worked with on *Licence to Kill*, *Titanic*, *The World is Not Enough* and *Die Another Day*. Our director was Martin Campbell, the early riser who had done such a good job on *GoldenEye*.

Nowhere in England had enough space for us at the time we wanted to shoot, so most of *Casino Royale* would be filmed in and around Prague, the capital of the Czech Republic. Interior sets were constructed at the city's Barrandov Studios. Before we started I met Steve Bohan, my new construction manager. I gave him the script and asked him to estimate the cost of the sets and dressing. He'd done a number of films in Prague, so I was confident I could trust his judgement. When he handed me his calculations I looked at the bottom line and said, "No way..." He immediately said, "Pete, I can't get it any lower than that without compromising the quality..." But I interrupted him. "Steve, I thought it would be double this figure!" On *Die Another Day* the art department had spent about $9 million, but Steve's estimate was somewhere between five and five-and-a-half. If I had any lingering doubts about filming in Prague they were immediately dispelled.

Along with Tony, Callum, the associate producer Andrew Noakes and a local production manager, I went on my first reconnaissance to the Czech Republic in 2005. This was a new environment for all of us, but I was acutely aware that the espionage thrillers *Mission: Impossible* (1996), *The Bourne Identity* (2002) and a large number of other films had been shot in Prague. We needed to present something fresh, so I suggested that rather than starting in Prague we should first go to Karlovy Vary, a spa town in western Bohemia. The location scout for *Ladyhawke* had taken me there over 20 years before, and I knew it looked quite different from Prague.

We arrived at the Grandhotel Pupp, where we were due to stay, and as soon as I saw the facade of the building I knew that we had found our location for the Hotel Splendide, the establishment in Montenegro where Bond shares a suite

FAR LEFT: The exterior of Casino Royale was the former Kaiserbad Spa in Karlovy Vary. The building was specially renovated for our purposes.

LEFT: Much of the film would follow Bond's activity in the casino.

BELOW LEFT AND RIGHT: Two views of the salon privé set at Barrandov. I decided to elevate this gaming table and add a handrail around the edge.

with his future lover Vesper Lynd (Eva Green). We didn't need to look much further for the exterior of Casino Royale itself, which was the former Kaiserbad Spa. We found this historic building in a sadly neglected state, so when we asked the local mayor if we could film there we offered to sponsor some restoration in exchange. He was very happy with our offer, and we paid the local preservation society to tart up the exterior on our behalf.

We tidied and redecorated the first floor, added revolving doors and a bar in the corner of the main room. Gaming tables were installed in the centre, but the salon privé – where the high rollers play for the biggest stakes – would be a set at Barrandov. The poker games at Casino Royale were crucial to the narrative. I knew that Martin would be spending a lot of time on these sets, so at Kaiserbad and Barrandov I decided to elevate the gaming tables. This wouldn't necessarily happen in a real casino, but I knew it would help us to avoid the kind of scene where the extras standing behind the gamers are cropped in order to get Bond and his opponents in shot. With a heightened seating area, the people standing around the tables would be the same height as those playing the games. We fitted a handrail around the seats to prevent the audience getting too close.

A thorough search of Prague resulted in a number of other locations. The black-and-white pre-titles sequence, where Bond earns his licence to kill, was partly filmed in a new office block called Danube House

RIGHT: The Skyfleet plane in its hangar. The plane was based on a Boeing 747, but customised with twin engines and wing tanks.

BELOW LEFT: With art department co-ordinator Sarah Robinson at Ruzyne Airport.

BELOW RIGHT: Concept art showing the exterior of the hangar.

in the Karlin District. I felt the glass lift and steel walkways provided a suitably stark backdrop to the brutally violent flashbacks.

When M (Judi Dench) is summoned to account for Bond's trigger-happy behaviour an establishing shot of the Houses of Parliament suggests we're in London, but her journey out of the committee rooms was actually filmed in the library of the Strhov Monastery. This location had also appeared in *From Hell* (2001), another film in which Prague had doubled for London.

Prague even stood in for Miami – the exterior of the Body Worlds anatomical exhibition was the Ministry of Transport, while the interior was filmed inside the Vitkov Monument mausoleum. Body Worlds was devised by Professor Gunther von Hagens, who appears in the film alongside exhibits that include a poker-playing trio of skinned cadavers. Sara Aghdami, one of my young assistants, spoke German so carried out the negotiations with the Professor on our behalf. Von Hagens' work divides opinion, and while many people consider it grotesque I find it fascinating.

Bond's efforts to save the Skyfleet plane at Miami Airport were a tapestry of scenes from different sources. The exterior of the main building was the as yet unopened Schengen terminal at Prague's Ruzyne Airport, but the runways were the aerodrome in Dunsfold, near Guildford, where the television series *Top Gear* is recorded.

Virgin Airlines' Richard Branson brought a brand new A340 Airbus to Prague, allowing us to use it as a prop that helped to create the impression that we were in an international airport. Richard also made a cameo in the film, being frisked by a customs officer.

Elsewhere at the airport, we adapted a huge prop of a Boeing 747 built by our aviation expert Mike Woodley. We gave it a completely different look – turning it into something more like a B52 – by adding twin engines to the inboard pylons and wing tanks to the outboard pylons. Shots of this prop were intercut with a model of the plane and its hangar made by my brother, Michael, and Steve Begg, the visual effects supervisor. Steve took pictures of the Airbus cockpit, its crew and various people on the ground, all of which were added digitally.

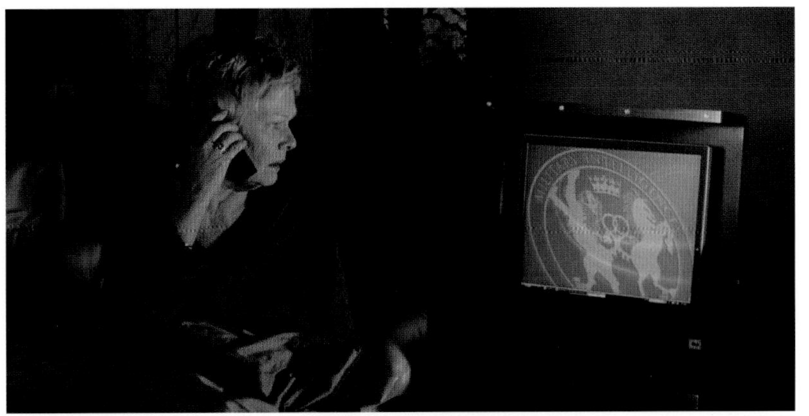

Far left: M (Judi Dench) is furious to find Bond lurking in her Canary Wharf penthouse.

Left: M is woken with news of Bond's progress and activates her bedside computer.

Below: The motorised drawers we added to the dashboard of Bond's Aston Martin.

Bottom: A close-up of the defibrillator that saves Bond's life.

The real aircraft took over once we got into the chase, although the planes taking off and landing in the background were Airfix models that Steve digitally integrated. He did a brilliant job.

There was an abundance of unusual buildings to film in, but it was still necessary to build quite a few sets at Barrandov. One of my favourites was M's home, which Bond breaks into. Martin asked me what I'd like to do with this set and we spent quite some time discussing it. I made the light-hearted point that we shouldn't make it look anything like the house Dame Judi's character occupied in her television sitcom *As Time Goes By*. Martin agreed, and then I said, "How about a penthouse in Canary Wharf?" I came up with an open-plan design that brought M into the recessed living area via a lift and several steps. Bond is waiting for her, perched on one of three Barcelona chairs positioned around a glass coffee table. Simon Wakefield dressed the set beautifully, and I was disappointed it wasn't retained for subsequent films.

I had already designed the main part of the flat when Martin told me he also wanted to set a scene in M's bedroom. We used faux leather and brass insets on the walls, and Simon placed a Japanese screen behind the bed. M's bedside table contained a computer screen that flipped up at the touch of a button. We originally fitted black sheets on the bed, but when Martin and Judi came to look at the set Martin decided that the sheets were a bit too much. Judi seemed game, however, joking that the camera should pull back to reveal that she was in bed with Roger Moore!

We did a deal with Ford, Aston Martin's then parent company, to have Bond drive the new DBS V12 in the film. The story called for Bond to bring a gun with various accessories and the defibrillator that Vesper uses to revive him when he's poisoned by Le Chiffre (Mads Mikkelsen) at the casino. We managed to secrete all this gadgetry in drawers beneath the dashboard, but I began to regret the decision when the damn things kept popping out at inopportune moments. Special effects supervisor Chris Corbould and his merry men came to my rescue, fitting unseen telescopic aerials that extended and retracted the drawers with the aid of small electric motors.

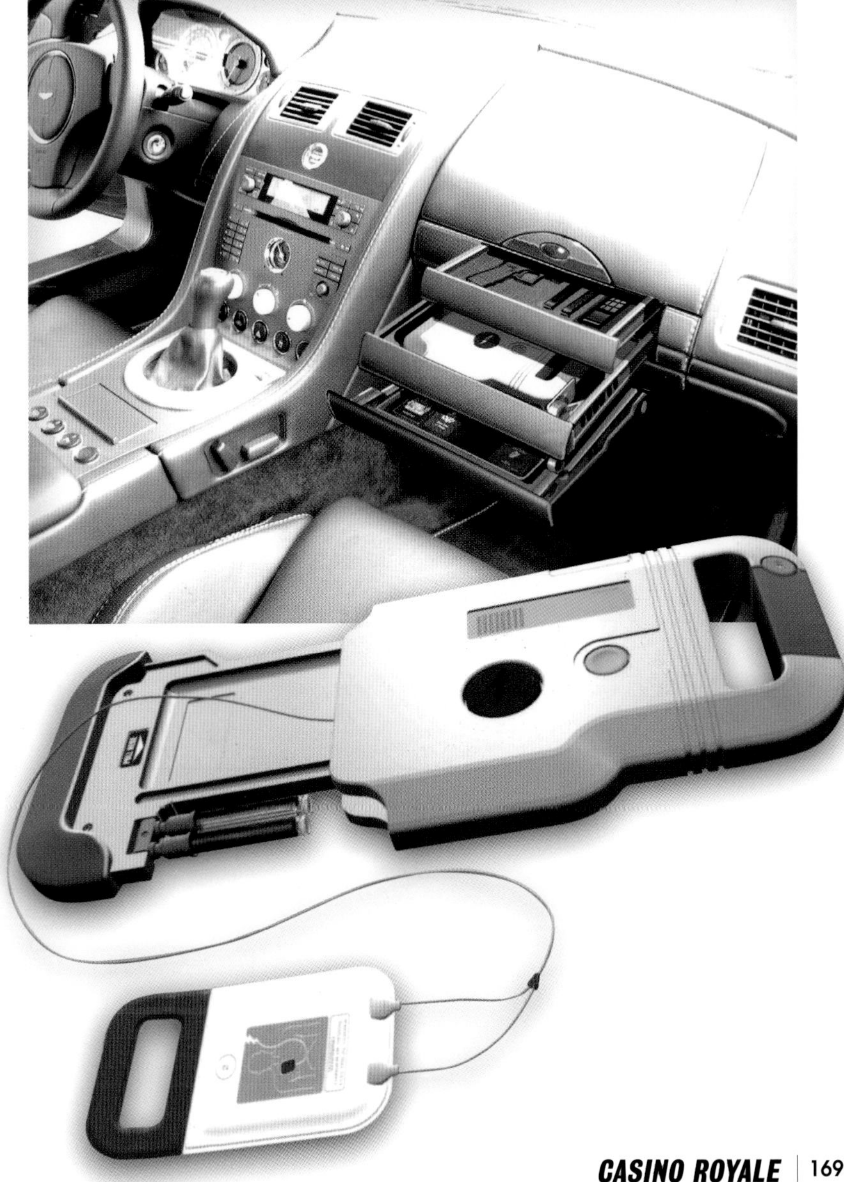

Right and below: Concept art of the rebel camp in Uganda.

Bottom: Exotic plants, red mud and a rain machine helped us to shoot this sequence in Black Park, near Pinewood.

The Czech Republic proved surprisingly adaptable, but we found locations in lots of other places too. The rebel camp in Uganda, seen straight after Daniel Kleinman's elegant opening titles, was shot at Black Park in Buckinghamshire. I'd been creating James Bond settings there since *Goldfinger* in 1964, and they knew that however much of a mess we made we'd always put things back the way they were. The script specified a jungle setting, which we achieved with a little help from a company called Living Props. It's amazing what can be achieved with some exotic plants, a liberal supply of red mud and a rain machine.

The freerunning chase between Bond and the bomb-maker Mollaka (Sébastien Foucan) was set in Madagascar. Sébastien is the founder of the freerunning sport, and he gave us one of the most breathtaking demonstrations of human agility I've ever seen. The sequence posed a major challenge, however – where would we find a location that could accommodate its sheer scale? We had already covered a lot of ground in our research for this film, going to Electric Mountain in Wales (where Martin had shot *Edge of Darkness*), South Africa (twice), Mozambique, all over Eastern Europe and round the Yugoslavian coast, and still we couldn't think of anywhere. I was the one who eventually suggested the Bahamas, because the chase traversed a building site and I recalled from the making of *The Spy Who Loved Me* in 1976 that a partly built hotel had been abandoned in Coral Harbour on New Providence Island.

I went there with Tony, Callum and Andrew. We stayed at the One & Only Club in Paradise Island, where butlers showed us to our bungalows. There was a sharp contrast between the luxury of the club and the decaying construction site at Coral Harbour. After nearly 30 years of neglect, the place was even worse than I remembered. A fire had burned what survived of the hotel and the pool was full of rubbish.

Martin and Michael Wilson then came out and they agreed that the site had potential. Michael very kindly held one end of a tape measure for me while I wrote down the dimensions of the place, and back in England Julian Caldow, one of my concept artists, created illustrations based on my notes and a digital fly-through of the route Sébastien would take.

Returning to Coral Harbour we tidied the place up and dressed it to resemble an active construction site once more. A couple of sheds housed the art department and the production office, while on the site itself we added a framework of structural steel and two tower frames. We were progressing well when Hurricane Katrina devastated New Orleans in the last week of August 2005. Work was interrupted when it became impossible to hire any cranes in the Bahamas because they had understandably been diverted to help with the rescue effort. We ended up erecting the towers using cranes we brought over from the UK.

When we eventually finished, I watched Sébastien choreographing his journey up, down and around the set, traversing huge sections of structural steel with remarkable precision. He would have happily jumped from one crane to the other without any safety wires, but that was more than our insurance company would allow.

In the preceding sequence, Bond and the inept Carter (Joseph Millson) identify Mollaka while hiding in the audience for a fight between a snake and a mongoose. This was filmed literally down the road from the construction site, in the empty space that had been intended for the hotel's swimming pool. A restaurant elsewhere in the Bahamas gave us the exterior of the African embassy where Bond finally kills Mallaka.

Above left: Bond pursues the bomb-maker Mollaka across a building site in Madagascar.

Above right: Mollaka was played by the freerunner Sébastien Foucan. The sequence was largely shot on a specially adapted set in the Bahamas.

Below left and right: Concept art and a still from the sequence where Le Chiffre (Mads Mikkelsen) subjects the naked Bond to excruciating torture.

Above left: We found the location for Mr White's sinister-looking house at a peninsula on Lake Como in Italy.

Above centre and right: Models of the sinking house in Venice.

Below left: The tracking device and its case.

Below right: Bond places his arm inside the moving scanner.

The film's Italian shoot included sequences filmed at Lake Como, where Bond convalesces from his torture and later catches up with the sinister Mr White (Jesper Christensen). We also went to Venice to film the exterior of the Canal Grande, the palazzo that sinks in the final act. We returned to Pinewood to film the collapse of the building, as the 007 Stage was the only place big enough for what we had in mind. We began by damming the tank into three compartments – one third would contain a full-size version of the sinking house, one third would contain a set of just the top of the house, and the largest compartment contained a set of the palazzo. The tank was around eight foot deep, but we topped the water up in the first two compartments to a depth of 12-15 feet.

The nature of the set-up meant you had to walk over one of the compartments to get into the set of the full-size house. Everyone griped about this at the time, but there was no other way to do it – any entrance built into the tank itself would have been useless once it was filled with water.

Computer-generated images enhanced the exterior of the house and the water, but the interior of the full-size house was made for real. I was chiefly inspired by the various levels and staircases in the Danieli, a five-star hotel near St Mark's

LEFT: The quarter-size model of the sinking house in the paddock tank at Pinewood.

BELOW: The house collapses into the water in a scene from the film.

BOTTOM: The tragic Vesper (Eva Green) locks herself into a lift in the sinking building.

Square. I roughed out my designs and Alan Tomkins, one of the art directors, drew up the plans. The set was built in sections at Pinewood, but some of the decorations came from Prague.

The carpenters and plasterers assembled the sets of the houses, which were placed onto hydraulic rigs that made them wobble before lowering them into the water. The original plan to shoot the destruction of the house in stages was altered when Martin decided to shoot the full-size house as one, continuous set. Ultimately we didn't use the top half at all. The results were a magnificent, and moving, climax to the picture.

The saga of the collapsing house didn't end there. Pinewood's fire department drained the tank, before an outside contractor moved in to break the sets up using acetylene cutters. From what I understand, a spark from one of the cutters ignited some dry wood on the set we never used. On 30 July 2006 the 007 Stage burned down. Again. Luckily there were no casualties and filming of *Casino Royale* was complete. The decision to rebuild was taken the very next day, and the damaged remnants of the stage were cleared in September. From its ashes rose a superstage, more sophisticated and versatile than either of its predecessors. It's still there.

Casino Royale opened to outstanding business in November 2006. I was delighted with the film, and especially pleased that Daniel's detailed performance as Bond won such acclaim from the critics. The series had renewed itself once more, with the most radical reinvention in its history. This was the beginning of an exciting new era for Bond. For me, however, an era was drawing to a close.

When we made *Casino Royale* there was talk of doing something we'd never attempted before and making the next film, *Quantum of Solace*, back to back. I had hoped to stay with the production, especially if Martin Campbell was going to direct. He had brought more than a touch of the *GoldenEye* magic to *Casino* and I enjoyed working with him enormously.

Quantum of Solace would prove to be a standalone production, and a new director, Marc Forster, was assigned. In spring 2007 Eon flew me out to Los Angeles for a meeting with Marc. It didn't go particularly well. I sensed that he was wary of working with someone who was 40 years his senior. Perhaps more seriously, I think he suspected I would be more sympathetic to the producers than to him. My loyalty to Michael and Barbara was beyond question, and I believe they wanted me to work on the picture, but ever since Cubby had promoted me to production designer I had always been chosen by the director and I'd worked for him. I was never a producer's man – I tried to help everybody.

I respected Marc's feelings, but told him that if I was to leave the Bond series I didn't want to hear it from anyone other than Michael and Barbara. They were kind enough to call me in for a chat, where they explained the films were moving on without me.

The Royal Film Performance
World Premiere of
CASINO ROYALE

ACCESS TO LEICESTER SQUARE - IMPORTANT INFORMATION

TRAFFIC INSTRUCTIONS:
If you are travelling by car or by taxi please note that you will need to be dropped off at the point indicated on the map and continue to the premiere entrance on foot (please see 'On Arrival' below). Please note that the traffic on the night of the premiere around Leicester Square will be heavily congested. Please allow ample time for your journey.

PARKING AND CAR PARKS:
No street parking is available in the immediate vicinity of Leicester Square, however, there are five NCP car parks nearby: NCP Brewer Street, NCP Denman Street, NCP Upper St. Martins Lane, NCP Swiss Centre, NCP Wardour Street.

BY TUBE:
The nearest tube stations are Leicester Square and Piccadilly Circus.

PEDESTRIANS:
The film is being premiered in the Odeon Leicester Square, the Odeon West End and the Empire Cinema. Guests for all three cinemas will enter the premiere via the gardens in Leicester Square. There is only one entrance to the gardens, this is closest to the Swiss Centre in Leicester Square.

ON ARRIVAL:
Please have your ticket wallet ready to show security. Please do not remove your cinema ticket from your wallet as the colour of the wallet indicates which cinema you will be directed to by security. Please take the time to familiarise yourself with the map on the reverse of these instructions in order to speed your entry to the correct cinema.

LEAVING THE CINEMA:
Please note that it is not possible for you to be collected by car from outside the cinema after the film.

EON

BELOW LEFT: *Casino Royale* premiered at London's Leicester Square Odeon on 14 November 2006.
BELOW RIGHT: My ticket to the event.

Dennis Gassner designed *Quantum of Solace* and has continued in that role for *Skyfall* (2012) and *SPECTRE* (2015). I had first met him in 1990, when his wife, Amy Ness, was the location manager for *Eve of Destruction*. A couple of years later Dennis won a richly deserved Oscar for his work on *Bugsy* (1991). I knew Dennis and Amy well, and I thought Dennis was an excellent choice.

In July 2007 I was on holiday in France with Ann when I received the news that Michael, by brother, had died of cancer. Michael had worked alongside me since *Goldfinger*, contributing models, foreground miniatures and other enhancements to the Bond films. He was a master of his craft, and in a way the brilliance of his work meant his talent was often unrecognised on screen. His death came as a terrible blow, and in the following months Ann would return to the subject of my retirement. This time I conceded that the moment had finally come to call it a day.

Ann and I travelled the world together over the next nine years, and when she passed away in January 2015 I lost the most important part of my life. It has been difficult coping without her, but the house never seems empty for long as we're a close family and I enjoy frequent visits from my children, grandchildren, and nephews, some of whom – as you will have read – followed me into the film business.

My own career in that business has come to an end, but I'm proud of the work I did and look back with nothing but fondness. They say that if you're lucky enough to find a job you enjoy then you'll never work again. When I reflect on the time I spent with Eon Productions, I can only conclude that for many years I was a very lucky man.

Above right: I was presented to the Queen at the premiere.

Above left: With my wife Ann, after the screening.

REFERENCES

Bond By Design: The Art of the James Bond Films by Meg Simmonds (Dorling Kindersley, 2015)
For My Eyes Only: Directing the James Bond Films by John Glen with Marcus Hearn (BT Batsford, 2001)
James Bond: The Legacy by John Cork and Bruce Scivally (Boxtree, 2002)
Ken Adam: The Art of Production Design by Christopher Frayling (Faber and Faber, 2005)
Kiss Kiss Bang! Bang! by Alan Barnes and Marcus Hearn (BT Batsford, 2000)
The Making of GoldenEye by Garth Pearce (Boxtree, 1995)
The Making of Licence to Kill by Sally Hibbin (Hamlyn, 1989)
Not Forgetting James Bond by Syd Cain (GBU, 2002)
The World is Not Enough: A Companion by Iain Johnstone (Boxtree, 1999)

Thanks also to the editors of *From Sweden With Love* (www.jamesbond007.se), *MI6: The Home of James Bond 007* (www.mi6-hq.com) and *The Worldwide Guide to Movie Locations* (www.movie-locations.com).

ACKNOWLEDGEMENTS

My thanks to Sally Geeson, who gave me the idea for this book, and Sean Robinson, who offered encouragement. Max Pemberton helped to initiate the project and came up with the title. Sarah Appleton carried out much of the transcription and Jonathan Rigby made valuable comments on the manuscript. My daughter Madelaine made corrections on my behalf, with help from my son Neil and grandchildren Ashley, Olivia and William.

Andy Boyle, Matthew Field, Gareth Owen and Vipul Patel helped with the picture research, and Mike Penny at Eon offered technical advice.

Marcus Hearn worked alongside me on the manuscript – I couldn't have done this without him – and Mike Jones designed the book. Thank you both for your patience, support and creativity.

A note for all the British crews I worked with. There are too many of you to name, but you know who you are. I have only been as good as the people who worked with me, and you were the very best. Thank you.

A mention for my American friends and colleagues. For Jim and John, Stephanie and Scott, and especially my lovely agents Robin and Jane. For Ned, Teri Ann and Bill Rae, Michael, Charles, Cindy and John, Robin and Lenny, and Diana. We've had some great times together.

I'd like to thank the late Cubby and Dana, Barbara and Michael for being part of the family. I enjoyed every moment, and we had a lot of success. Their colleagues at Eon (both of today and yesteryear) have also been so kind to me over the years: Reg Barkshire, Anne Bennett, Bill Cartlidge, Callum McDougall, Andrew Noakes, the late Doug Noakes, the late Tom Pevsner, David Pope, Emma Reynolds, the late Harry Saltzman, Meg Simmonds, Stanley Sopel, Tony Waye, Greg Wilson and everyone in the PR and marketing departments. My thanks also to all the directors I worked with on the Bond films.

Finally, a special mention for some of the crew members who have passed on: Ernie Archer, Charlie Bishop, Syd Cain, Teddy Carrick, Maurice Carter, Peter Childs, Lionel Couch, Carmen Dillon, Roy Dorman, Fred Hole, my brother Michael, Jack Maxsted, Derek Meddings, Jim Morahan, Peter Murton, Harry Pottle, Tony Rimmington, Ronnie Udell, 'Vetch' and most recently Sir Ken Adam, who was my mentor for many years. I miss you all.